A Secular Sobriety©

*Including
a secular version of the first 164 pages
of the Big Book*

by

Dale K.

Second Edition

© 2017 Dale K. All rights reserved

Dedication

To Henry H. (aka Henry Half Measure) who was often cantankerous and disagreeable, but always a good friend. Sometimes I cringed, but most often I laughed and learned. Through good and bad examples, Henry taught me about sobriety and how to be an atheist within AA. Thank you for co-founding the Boca Raton We Agnostics Group. It was my lifesaver over the years. I miss you dearly.

Also, to my daughter, Rebecca, who is the most authentic person I know. Your example encourages me to be the same. Thank you for your inspiration and teaching your Dad a thing or 12.

Acknowledgements

Members of my home group received copies of my book after it was first published. Two members returned the following week and made offers to proofread it for me. One was a proofreader for the local newspaper. The other was a retired English teacher. I had no idea that I had friends with such talents. Their corrections were very humbling.
It was painfully obvious that I didn't pay much attention in school. My apologies to the nuns that tried their best.

Mostyn T. and Susan G. did an excellent job of refining my book for this second edition. Their time was very much appreciated. Their education, experience, talents and suggestions have made this a much better book. As a result, the book can serve its readers better. I am very pleased with the wonderful and important work that they have done. I will always be grateful for their generous contributions.

Thank you!

Contents

Introduction...1

Cultural Complacency..7

Longing To Belong..21

A Look Within...29

Running The Gauntlet...37

A Solution For All..49

More Concerning Alcoholism......................................65

For The Agnostic..81

How It May Work...95

Taking Action..113

Helping Others..133

To The Spouse...149

To The Family...169

To The Employer..185

A Vision For All..201

Stories And Appendices......................................219

Conclusion...237

Personal Secular Stories

Joy!...243

Alli O...247

Elisabeth H...251

Ed S..255

Tomas L...259

Introduction

Hello. My name is Dale and I'm an alcoholic. Also, I'm what many call an atheist. That label is for you. I don't find a personal label necessary. In fact, I don't like the term. It has too much negativity connected to it. I'm not anti-theist. I couldn't care less what others believe. In fact, I'm a believer, too! I believe in science. That ever-growing knowledge of this place I live in and how I fit into it. That's wonderfully positive! There is plenty of emotion that colors my thoughts, but my core beliefs are science based. I really don't need a label for all this. I'm just a guy struggling through life like everyone else. Much of what I hold to be true is a temporary truth. With time, new discoveries will shed light on new truths that may also be temporary. The one truth that I believe to be permanent is love. So, if you must label me, call me a lover.

January 6, 2018 was my 37th anniversary of sobriety. I don't say this to boast. I say it because I think you should know my qualifications for writing this. During my early days in AA, it seemed like I was the only skeptic in a sea of religious disciples. I was told that my lack of faith was an obstacle in the way of sobriety. "You shouldn't worry though," they said. "Soon enough you will get it." In the meantime, I could use their higher power. I was told that would be sufficient until I found my own. The expression "fake it until you make it" was offered as hope that even this heathen could find sobriety with the god "of my own understanding."

After a considerable test of time, it was realized that I wasn't going to "get it." My sponsor arranged a meeting for me with a man they described as the "Resident Agnostic." This person was in a city 30 miles away, so I assumed there was only one in all of South Florida. He was very friendly and considerate. He was a writer for the local newspaper and I enjoyed discussing the "god" element of AA with him. Essentially, he told me that his solution was to add an "o" every time he heard or read the word god. This changed god to good. It made sense to me and I was convinced that I had my answer.

This was a good (pun intended) beginning for me. As I journeyed into sobriety, this simple translation worked well most of the time. Sometimes it didn't work at all. There were moments when I wondered if I would ever find all this good without finding god. Seemingly, everyone else in AA believed in a god. The peer pressure was formidable, to say the least.

Shortly after my first year of sobriety, I decided that I would take a closer look at religion. It was recommended that I read William James' *The Varieties of Religious Experience* and also the Bible. I realized that I had great disdain for a book that I had never read. This falls under the "contempt prior to investigation" category. While reading the Bible, I decided I had contempt during investigation. I read about so much wickedness, violence and terrible things in the Old Testament. Then, in the New Testament, I found less evil, but it still fell way short of satisfying. Finally, I read John 4:16. It said something that hit me like a bolt of lightning! "God is love!" Holy shit! I mean…literally…**HOLY** shit!!! I didn't need to read more. I closed the book and never opened it again. I found the answer I was looking for. God isn't just good. That was okay, but inadequate. God is love.

Finally, I had my "Spiritual Experience." It was sudden and profound. It was lovely! I had the biggest grin on my face. This was my epiphany. Oddly enough the Epiphany (a Christian holiday) is the same as my sobriety date. I remember sleeping like a baby that night. The next day, I decided that whatever I was doing, whatever decision I had to make, I would ask myself a simple question: "What is the loving thing?" The next day, I gave love a test run. My day full of love was the best day I have ever had. I try to have that day again but, of course, life and my humanity are constant barriers. Life is a complicated endeavor. Often, simplistic answers aren't enough. Love is a very large subject. Many of the details are common and obvious. Many more are hidden in the folds, crevices and secrets that make our journey through life challenging and fascinating. Finding your humble self will be your best friend in this discovery of who you are in sobriety.

The irony of an atheist finding answers in the Bible is not lost on me. There are many dichotomies in my life. I welcome them. In fact, I love them. They're an indication of open-mindedness. That quality will be most helpful in your quest for a sober life. We must be open to all that is around us. Many things you examine will be dismissed, but we must consider all of it. Take a little of this and a bit of that and create this unique sober person that will be beautiful to you. Be genuine. Be who you are. Own yourself. Try not to worry about what others might think. They are not living your life and have plenty of problems of their own. And, while you're trying to ignore those that may judge, don't judge others. Let them have their lives just as you wish to have yours. This is the essence of serenity.

I would like to address the AA principle of "contempt prior to investigation." It is very difficult to investigate what AA has to offer non-believers if you can't read past all the references to a deity. Far too many non-believers have too much difficulty with this. The easy reaction is to dismiss AA and its members. That rejection means you will not find the beauty and wisdom of the program and the wonderful sober people that have come before you on this journey of sobriety. Don't be blinded by contempt. Certainly, the Big Book can be quite obnoxious and arrogant. Don't allow the book's problems to become yours. An open mind will allow you to hear the bits of wisdom that help you on this wonderful experience of life without alcohol or other drugs. And remember, the only truth is the one you accept for yourself. Truth wears many clothes. Your truth does not mean another's different truth is wrong. Both are right (and wrong). As you wish to be accepted and respected for your beliefs and who you are, extend that same acceptance and respect to others.

This is a quote by Adyashanti. "Make no mistake about it. Enlightenment is a destructive process. It has nothing to do with becoming better or being happier. Enlightenment is the crumbling away of untruth. It's seeing through the facade of pretense. It's the complete eradication of everything we imagine to be true." Now, I don't give a rat's behind about spiritual gurus, but this quote speaks to the notion that all is true and untrue at the same time. If you understand how science works, you will understand the fluidity of truth. Also, keep in mind that we should not be satisfied with mere enlightenment. When we apply our newfound enlightenment, we get the better and happier parts, too!

Many times during our lives we, will determine that what we know is true. As we mature in sobriety, we will find new truths that displace old truths. Truth is a very dynamic thing. That which works for us today may not work tomorrow. An open mind, eyes and ears will allow us to find our new truths. This is the enlightenment which feeds our serenity and happiness. This is the foundation of my sobriety and a meaningful life.

Cultural Complacency

There are as many paths to sobriety as there are people seeking it. I won't pretend to know if one way is better than another. I will say, however, the path that works for you is **your** best way. You have to become your own expert. While learning from others who have more knowledge and experience is important, you have to evaluate this information and decide what works best for you. My way was in AA. I can only share my experience. This was not an effortless or uncomplicated path. I struggled with how this spiritual program could be adapted to my secular life. There was no road map for this. Other AA members were of little help. According to them, a higher power was god, period. It was only a matter of how one understands *Him*. Yes, the upper case "H" is ever present. When the Big Book was written, even god's gender wasn't an option. This is 80-year-old thinking. Because of those prevailing attitudes, my atheism stayed on the "down low" for some time. There are plenty of great ideas and much wisdom in the book *Alcoholics Anonymous*. Unfortunately, as a non-believer, it's difficult to see past all the religiosity and condescension to discover this wisdom. But, that is exactly what we are going to do. Hopefully I will show you how to look past those things that don't pertain to atheists so you can see the nuggets of wisdom that are pertinent in the Big Book.

After about seven years of sobriety, I heard someone mention an AA meeting called "We Agnostics." With great hope, I cornered that guy after the meeting. I had no idea there was such a thing in AA. I had to find out the where and when of it.

Quite honestly, I was anticipating and looking forward to a lot of god bashing at this meeting. I had a lot of anger about how the god thing made AA so difficult and inconvenient for me. I received quite a surprise at that first meeting. The discussion subject was, of all things, gratitude! What the hell? After years of suffering in silence, I wanted some good-old god bashing, god dammit! That was my first lesson from this group. There is no need for god bashing. I needed to rid myself of any resentments I had for AA's cultural lag. I'm sure that AA would disagree with this sentiment, but there is very little evidence to the contrary in their current literature. I'll discuss this cultural lag in more detail throughout the book.

This meeting was not just composed of agnostics and atheists. Some of them believed in a god. The big difference from regular AA meetings was that they made no reference to a deity or religion. All of that was left outside the room. The focus of these meetings was on sobriety and all the "living problems" we needed to overcome in order to stay sober. Some members of the group were quite rebellious and wanted little, if anything, to do with AA's Big Book or program. They were content to figure it all out for themselves. I am not that type of person. I have no interest in total revolution. These individuals had an extremely negative view of AA and wanted no part of AA's program. A partial revolution with a "live and let live" attitude is much better suited to my essential need for serenity. I'm happy to listen to others that have come before me and those that came after. Their experiences and knowledge are invaluable. I will consider their opinions and how they might fit into my life. I might reject them, but I will try to listen and consider them. I don't believe any person can figure this out on his or her own. Sharing and listening with respect are part of a healthy community. This community (AA refers to it as fellowship) is vastly important to my sobriety. I don't think I need to reinvent the wheel. I just need to improve on it and keep it relevant to me as an individual.

I learned that sobriety was as uncomplicated as not picking up a drink. But then, if you don't pick up that drink, you create a new problem. Now you have a living problem. How will I live without drinking? AA's answer is to live a spiritual life. I wanted that spirituality without having to accept belief in a deity to achieve it. Religion does not have the corner on the ethics market. A virtuous life is accessible to all who seek it. All you need to recognize the difference between right and wrong is a conscience. As we remain sober, we develop a new relationship with our conscience. With very few exceptions, everyone's conscience works quite well. Sometimes we bullshit ourselves so we will feel better about doing wrong. That doesn't mean we're right. Add a good dash of empathy and all sorts of kindness and virtue will follow!

It was very important and timely that I discovered people that were on the same page as I was. This gave me a better sense of community. In regular AA meetings, I felt like a bit of an outsider. AA provides two things that I find to be very important to my sobriety. Fellowship and a well-organized program of recovery are the two cornerstones of Alcoholics Anonymous. If I can combine my desire and effort for sobriety with those things, I create a nurturing environment and a kind of behavior that gives me a sound path to quality sobriety. The likelihood of a sober and gratifying life increases exponentially with acceptance from people you attend AA meetings with.

Let's examine that cultural lag I wrote of earlier. Alcoholics Anonymous was founded in 1935. In the earliest time, it involved the Oxford Group, a non-denominational movement modeled after extreme Christianity. The group's secret ingredient was what they described as god control. To Bill Wilson's credit, it took him less than two years to separate Alcoholics Anonymous from these people. From this time forward, AA has made the claim that it doesn't support any specific religion, but it holds fast and steady to a supernatural being. And, without question, it is a very Christian god. Nonetheless, they give members the leeway of a "higher power of their own understanding," but this higher power is always upper case. Lower case higher powers are laughed at and "in time" all will understand HP to be God…right? (wink, wink). This attitude is condescending at best. At the worst, it is an indignity to people who don't believe in gods or whose god is not the Christian god. If not completely repulsed, these people find it discouraging to continue attending AA meetings as they become, more and more, marginalized by the Christians. I certainly did. I often wonder what would have happened if I had not found the We Agnostics meeting in Boca Raton. I may not have fallen off the wagon, but I'm certain my personal growth would have been slowed.

AA is not keeping current with today's diverse culture. There are a lot of Christians in the U.S., but their numbers are decreasing. The number of people with no religion or belief in supernatural beings is increasing. AA is struggling against this tide of non-believers. They see secular members as a threat to AA and its Christian dogma. In many ways, they act like the Oxford Group of times past. They condemn rigid, close-minded thinking for newcomers, but practice it themselves. Making changes so that all alcoholics will feel welcome is a good thing. I know change is difficult, but it's critical for personal growth. AA has beat that into my head. The organization of AA does not behave like they insist (suggest) the members should.

The book *Alcoholics Anonymous* was first published in 1939. Subsequent editions were published in 1955, 1976 and 2001. Very little has changed. Most of the changes in the latest edition are in the personal stories. The first 164 pages, which describe the recovery program, changed a teensy bit early on. Recently, there have been no changes to this portion. All of my comments regarding page numbers or quotes from *Alcoholics Anonymous* are referencing the Fourth Edition (2001).

In the Foreword to the Fourth Edition, AA states that from 1976 to 2001, "worldwide membership has just about doubled, to an estimated two million or more, with almost 100,800 groups meeting in approximately 150 countries around the world." As of 2012, the Big Book has been translated into 64 languages and there are over 108,000 groups in about 170 countries with an estimated membership well over two million. AA must be one of the most diverse groups in the world. I'm not convinced it recognizes this diversity. It may be that AA believes this growth is because of, rather than in spite of, its Christian ways. Perhaps they think they are doing a wonderful thing by converting all the world to Christianity. If so, they have lost their way. Religious conversion is not the primary mission of Alcoholics Anonymous and it shouldn't be its secondary mission either. I believe its insistence on retaining the strong Christian culture, that is today's AA, will eventually result in a very unwanted backlash. I hope AA will survive it and promote a more open culture.

With all of AA's collective wisdom gained over the course of 80 years of sobriety and personal growth, most would think it would recognize this diversity. Maybe AA just chose to ignore it. If something works for you, it's easy to think it will work for everybody. "If I got sober this way, it must be the right way for everyone," the thinking goes. Unfortunately, this attitude does not consider diversity and individualism. We say, "Easy Does It," but easy is not what we're here for. By not recognizing and taking significant steps to include everyone, regardless of background, culture or beliefs, AA is taking the easy way out. It is being lazy. AA needs to get out of its comfort zone. "Wouldn't life be grand if we were all white and Christian," AA seems to be implying with each new edition of *Alcoholics Anonymous*. I do hope that is wrong, but I don't think I'm too far off the mark. I'm certain that others will feel compelled to attack my opinion. I will welcome the criticism and I look forward to beginning a well-needed conversation. But, please keep in mind, I'm asking for a conversation. If all you want is an argument, I won't be participating in that. AA should be as diverse as the world it serves, so that all who seek sobriety, may find it without prejudice.

There are many barriers to the acceptance of diversity. Prejudice and stereotyping are major problems. The notion that one's beliefs are the only "true" beliefs creates an attitude that people with other beliefs are wrong and inferior. Believing others are somehow less than you allows for hatred and prejudice. People tell themselves stories about how these lesser people live or think. Sometimes they believe others are evil. Treating these people poorly seems to be okay if a person has convinced themselves that others are so inferior. Some on the fringes of extremism believe their god hates these other people.

Cultural expectations get in our way, too. When I moved to this rural area, with its monoculture, everyone just assumed I was Christian like them. "Isn't everybody?," is how the thinking goes. When they find out otherwise, all sorts of fear and defensiveness come to the front. "You're different?" "How different?" "Are you going to threaten my way of life?" "Do you think you are better than me?" "Two different beliefs?" "One must be right and the other wrong!" "Fight against new ideas!" This kind of fear is born of ignorance. The answers for this type of ignorance are curiosity, knowledge and understanding. Resistance to new things just deepens your ignorance. Eliminating the fear of other cultures is the first step towards acceptance and a genuinely honest and open fellowship in AA.

Resistance to change is enormous. "We've been doing it this way forever!" "If it was good enough for the old-timers in AA, it's good enough for me!" "Who the hell does this guy think he is … coming in here and saying those things that aren't in the Big Book?"

The thing about diversity is that it's coming, whether anyone likes it or not. If you don't like it, you can go deeper into the woods to avoid it. Another option is to welcome it. Try to understand the benefits of diversity. At the very least you will hear different points of view. Who knows? Maybe you'll learn something new!

Think of diversity like economics. A closed economic system means there is no new or outside money entering the system. Everybody is just selling each other hamburgers (so to speak). The system stagnates and weakens. Eventually it must implode because some refuse to spend any more money on hamburgers. An open system is one where new money is entering the system. The economy is healthy and thrives because new money causes growth and variety. The diversity in the economy means you can buy more than just a hamburger. Diversity has the same effect on thoughts, ideas and societies. Some old ideas are good and should remain. Others are past their prime and, if kept, will have a negative effect on innovation and growth. Even AA's program believes we should have personal growth for sobriety. There is nothing scary about foregoing ground beef for a Porterhouse steak once in a while.

I certainly understand the sentimentality of retaining the originality of AA's historical book. I'm a very sentimental person and I get it. It is a direct link to AA's founders and their thoughts about how to stay sober. The original version is nothing short of historical and precious! It should remain this way. I even think Chapter 4, "We Agnostics," should remain. If for nothing else, it can be a consistent reminder of the lack of acceptance for diverse thought and cultures that used to be.

However, I believe AA should emphasize how wrong this chapter is in the next edition. AA's program teaches: "When we are wrong, promptly admit it." There is no shame in being wrong. The shame is when you refuse to admit it and refuse to change. Willful ignorance should never be acceptable. I have no desire to change the underlying program of AA. It certainly has worked for me and I believe in it. However, I believe wording in the Big Book should change to be more inclusive. AA should also encourage its members to be more inclusive.

AA is being populated by many alcoholics that are not white or Christian. Every ethnicity, culture, race and religion is becoming a part of AA. Many Christians will see my attitude as an attack on them. When you are a member of a privileged group, suggesting equality can seem like an attack. It is not. Requesting equal respect and acceptance for other groups is what it is. It is nothing more. There is no hidden agenda. It's just respect and acceptance. All the Christians can remain Christian. I don't want to take anything away from AA. I want to add something. I want to add acceptance, understanding and respect for diverse people. That certainly doesn't sound very threatening to me.

As in our personal sobriety, AA should move forward without forgetting the past. We don't dwell or live in the past and AA shouldn't either. Alcoholics Anonymous should move forward by being more inclusive, welcoming and understanding towards all. There is no reason for AA to be in the business of converting non-believers or non-Christians.

Diversity offers enormous benefits, also. I find the easiest way

I can learn things is to listen to someone that has a different perspective. I recently heard a quote from Bill Nye: "Everyone you will ever meet, knows something you don't." I love that idea! If you could just sit back and think about that for a while you would have to come out the other end a better person. It inspires me to listen and be kind while interacting with others. That allows me to hear what they know. I must actively listen. By that I mean, I must try to put personal emotions aside and hear what is being said from the speaker's perspective. If I listen in the context of my perspective, I can only hear with biased ears. My biased ears will, more than likely, misunderstand.

I came to AA because I can't do this on my own. I can't do all my own thinking. Listening to the same thing being regurgitated over and over helps to get things to sink in and be remembered, but you have to mix things up. You have to hear and be willing to entertain new ideas. You have to be humble and open-minded enough to know that things you believe might be wrong. If you're not willing to be open to new ideas, you will never grow. I cannot just adapt to AA's way of thinking and then stop. There is wisdom to be found outside the rooms of AA, too. Likewise, as an institution, AA cannot believe it is the acme of all necessary thought regarding sobriety. AA must continue to change and grow just as it teaches us to. Welcoming and respecting the diversity among AA members is crucial for that to develop. Changing something as successful as AA should be mindful and deliberate. Slow, of course, but AA's pace is more like stagnation.

I would suggest, in the next edition of Alcoholics Anonymous, adding some honest understanding of other beliefs and cultures. I'm almost certain that there are active alcoholics that are a part of every religion on earth. Also, the number of non-believers is growing more and more. All these people should not be ignored or considered lesser members. They cannot continue to believe the chapter "We Agnostics" will suffice. That chapter is nothing less than demeaning to non-believers. All these people are seeking sobriety and they should feel included. Empathy and understanding of non-believers are virtues that need to be addressed by AA and its members. Helping everyone to find sobriety should be the bigger priority. Why should all but Christians struggle through the Big Book to figure out how this program can work for them? I know ... I know ... as you understand "Him." Using that as an answer to this problem is only making excuses for a lack of personal and organizational understanding of others.

I'll say it again. AA in the United States is very white and very Christian. I've attended AA meetings that set out pictures of Jesus along with posters of the 12 Steps and 12 Traditions. I don't wish to criticize a group like that. That helps them stay sober. If that's what works for them, great! However, this kind of group must understand that visitors and newcomers may be very turned off by these things. The group may decide it doesn't care about visitors or newcomers. That is certainly its choice. Every group is autonomous and should remain so. What I'm asking is that AA World Services, Inc. and individual AA members begin to recognize and embrace all of the existing and future members' beliefs. Many AA groups and individuals will refuse, but AA as a whole needs to encourage this attitude of respect and acceptance. Anything less should be no part of a spiritual program.

After 29 years of sobriety, I sold my business, retired and moved away from Boca Raton. I started to explore meetings near my new home. At one meeting I was told, "If you don't find Jesus, you will never stay sober." I felt sorry for the person who said that. I hope he finds a greater understanding and acceptance for those unlike him.

Also, where are all the black people? I'm sure that alcoholism affects them equally. I see very few in the meetings that I have attended. I've been to meetings all over the United States. Is there a separate, underground black AA that I'm unaware of? I hope so.

I'm not asking for an apology or fixing fault, but Alcoholics Anonymous World Services, Inc. and the AA General Service Board need to grow along with its worldwide membership. The spirit of AA must live on through its pioneers, but AA must begin to recognize that it has grown far beyond anything the pioneers could have imagined. I'm proud of and grateful for the AA pioneers and all who came before me. Those people are why AA was there for me when I was in need. Alcoholics Anonymous should evolve into the 21st century with the virtues of grace, empathy, acceptance and understanding. After all, a virtuous life is the essence of the AA program. This is how AA will continue to be there for all in need of sobriety.

I recently heard of a new AA clubhouse about 10 miles away. One day, I was in the area and decided to stop by. My only intention was to see where it was. After looking through the front window, I realized it was open. I went in and found myself in the middle of a Big Book meeting. I politely sat down and listened. After the meeting, I spoke to a man that I knew from my home group. He was one of those with very long sobriety and I always enjoyed listening to him. I decided to return the next week because he would be there.

I brought my old (third edition, 1979) Big Book with me. While they were reading aloud, I realized my book was different. When I asked about this, they said they were reading from a newer edition. I thought to myself, "They have a new edition?" I must admit that I had been too isolated from "regular" AA for too long. I was a dozen years late learning about the existence of this new edition. I bought a new Big Book and was very excited and eager to read it and see what was different. This was the fourth edition, printed in 2001. Perhaps my hopes were too high. I was quickly disappointed. The differences were very minor. The only things new were the "Forward to the Fourth Edition" and some new "Personal Stories." Chapters 1-11 were completely unchanged. I understand the great reluctance to change. The original text is considered by many to be divinely inspired. Sometimes it's referred to as the AA Bible. I wonder if, in the Middle East or Africa, Muslims refer to it as the AA Koran? Many would like everyone to believe it is divinely inspired. That, of course, is impossible for the secular person. At the very least, it is historical.

There have been some changes to the original 1939 text, so changes are not unprecedented. I agree that the essence of it should stay intact. But, I believe it needs to be expanded and/or changed to be more inclusive. I'm sure there is a sizable number of members that do not believe in worshiping a deity. Adding a new chapter, or even a paragraph, accepting non-believers, as they are, would be wonderful. Unfortunately, I don't think that will happen. Religious people seem to be afraid that if they accept and approve of non-believers, they are, in some way, negating their beliefs. I'm sure that is a poor explanation. It's difficult for me to explain it because I don't understand it. Tolerance, acceptance, understanding, comity and empathy are spiritual values. I just don't get it.

Longing To Belong

The very beginning of AA was a fellowship between two individuals. Two guys sharing their thoughts and desires. They leaned on each other for support in a very difficult time. This is the essence of what AA is. Depending on your sober condition or preferences, this could be the most important part of AA. In the beginning of my sobriety, it was everything. There are many who wish to go it alone, but I'm not one of them. Being part of a community of like-minded people and having friends that support your new way of life is, for me at least, vital to staying sober. There would be little need for meetings if this were not so. We, as humans, are very social animals. A sense of community, developed through social inclusion, is very important to the vast majority of us. This is the reason that I believe it is way beyond the time that AA, as an organization, and its members, as individuals, should open their hearts, minds and arms in welcoming atheists, agnostics, freethinkers and all of the secular drunks into the AA fellowship without trying to convert them into deists or think we are incapable of virtue because of our lack of belief in their god. The foundation of spirituality and virtue is a good sense of empathy. Religion can help with that, but religion is not a requirement for it. Claiming otherwise is nothing less than religious sales and marketing tactics.

In 2010 my wife and I moved to a town 60 miles away. Our new town was much smaller. Both of us grew up in small towns. We enjoy the quiet and slower pace. The down side was that this more rural place was much less multicultural and more religious. There was nothing like my old We Agnostics meeting there. We loved our new home, but my struggle to find a new AA meeting that I could call "home" was challenging. Sometimes I drove to my old meeting, but that was very impractical. A round-trip of 120 miles was time consuming and costly. I needed a local meeting. I hadn't been to a "regular" AA meeting in more than 20 years. This wasn't going to be fast or easy. After a while, I found a meeting with many members that had very long-term sobriety. At least half a dozen people had longer sobriety than I did. I never want to be the smartest person in the room, so all the longevity was a good beginning. There was plenty of talk about god, but I expected that and I accepted it. The really good things were the wisdom and serenity of these people. I became quite comfortable with my new home group. I even came to realize some were non-believers like me. Somehow, they figured out how to fit in without rocking the religious boat. Staying quiet and keeping their beliefs to themselves was a big part of their strategy.

I did the same for quite a long time. For whatever reason, I was very self-conscious about being different. I didn't want to be that new weird guy. I wanted acceptance. I even wondered if they believed my length of sobriety. I thought I would give things plenty of time and let them get to know me. I found much friendship and fellowship at this meeting. In time, some came to know me well. Some chose to keep a distance and that's okay, too. How others treat me is their path. How I react is mine. It is not my job to change the hearts and minds of others. My purpose at meetings is to grow my heart and mind and to share. Also, I had the help of a therapist. Her guidance helped tremendously. Finding my place in "normal" AA was not easy. I had all sorts of ugly and stupid thoughts that I knew were improper. I developed resentments towards some of the more religious members. I had far too many negative and critical thoughts. After many hours of conversation with the therapist, I was able to work through all of this. I came to understand that, because I wanted to be tolerated, I needed to be tolerant. And, to be honest, tolerance is just the first step. Trying to understand and accept people as they are is more the goal.

The other take-away from my therapy sessions was that I needed to be more genuine and worry less about what others think of me. I have a daughter that is very authentic. I use her example as a source of inspiration and strength. I need to be myself. And, so do you. If you're an atheist, be proud of that! I think atheists are about the last group of people with such a high percentage still in the closet. All the gays are out and getting married now. We are one of the last groups of people that it is still okay to hate. To judge someone on nothing more than their position regarding religion or gods is ridiculous. This is the land of freedom, liberty and strong individuals. It is time for us to be free and strong individuals. Be proud of yourself. Liberate yourself. Be genuine.

I would like to give a thumbs-up to the mental health profession. I'm a firm believer in the benefits of professional mental therapy. I believe it should be a regular part of our mental maintenance. We brush and floss our teeth to have fewer dental problems. We visit our primary physician for annual checkups. We eat well and exercise so we have fewer physical problems. Having conversations regarding spirituality with friends and going to AA meetings improves our spiritual fitness. In the same way, we should take care of our mental health. Maintenance is so much easier than fixing a problem after we are broken. If we learn how to think properly, when a problem does arise, we can deal with it more effectively and come out the other end in a much better place. We should be mindful of our physical, spiritual *and* mental health.

Alcoholics Anonymous is wonderful, but its members are amateurs in the mental health field. There is much wisdom in the rooms of AA. There is also much ignorance and stupidity. Keeping your ears and mind open will help you decide which is which. I would guess the population of AA is a very good cross section of the general population. It is full of very smart people, idiots and everything in-between. Your job is to recognize who is who. Also, keep in mind that today's idiot might be tomorrow's enlightened one. I have created a very unscientific theory. I call it the "Idiot Factor." The Idiot Factor suggests that, at any given moment, 48% of people are idiots. How I arrived at this number and the actual percentage is unimportant. This group of idiots is very dynamic. The people in that group fluctuate constantly. All of us, at some point, are part of the group. Some people stay in the group longer than others. After a while you can recognize the ebb and flow of this group like the tides of the ocean. Knowing that you, and all others, are an occasional part of it will keep you humble and respectful. Embrace wisdom when you hear it, but don't reject what you think is stupid until you've examined it thoroughly. Try to stay out of the idiot group as much as possible. The longer you are sober, the better your chances are.

Unfortunately, far too many people still believe atheists are the devil incarnate. At the very least some think we are under Lucifer's spell. I've heard that we not only worship the devil, but eat babies. At the very least, we are considered very angry! I spoke to a religious person about this. He believed we were angry at god. I asked him how this could be true, considering that we don't believe in god. He couldn't explain it. He just knew it was true. As an atheist or whatever, I plead with you to not feed that sort of stereotyping and prejudice. If you are militant or insult others by criticizing their beliefs, you're giving credence to that kind of thinking. In spite of the fact that many treat us negatively, please don't act the same. Don't be the "angry atheists" that they think we are. Don't play into these erroneous ideas. There is a big difference between challenging religious belief and expressing non-belief. Be a good example of a kind and compassionate non-believer. Respect for others and their beliefs will earn you respect for yours. Religions have been around for almost as long as humans. They are deeply ingrained into every society. Religions won't be going away anytime soon. If and when the present religions do go by the wayside, you can be certain that others will be created to fill the void. Religion and going to church fills a strong need for answers and being part of a community. AA works in much the same way, but the dynamics are different. At church, everyone is of the same belief. At AA, many different beliefs are represented. AA members should be like Unitarians. Mutual acceptance and respect will allow all AA members to have this strong sense of belonging that is so important to us and our sobriety.

The desire to be part of a group is as old as humankind. Other animals did it long before we came along. The origins of groups are rooted in survival. It is still very important for survival and has evolved to include our sense of well-being. Wanting to "fit in" starts at a very early age and never leaves the vast majority of people. We want to be accepted for who we are. Being included in a group makes us feel good about ourselves. It makes us feel safe. It's very comforting. There are ample reasons why we have so many groups, clubs, societies, churches, etc. The sense of belonging is very relevant to a healthy sense of self. AA's fellowship is an admirable example of this. Knowing that I'm not alone and that others are experiencing the same things I am helps me immensely in my quest for a sober life.

The AA community is where I've learned whatever it is I know about sobriety, serenity and a well-lived life. It is where I learned about whatever virtues I have today. No matter how intelligent I think I am, I know I could never have figured this out on my own. In fact, I've come to understand my intelligence has little to do with my recovery. What stands between me and a drink is developing the wisdom to practice virtue and protect my serenity. Quite honestly, I can't imagine sobriety without being a part of this group of other sober people. The fellowship of AA is central to my sobriety.

I have recently learned of a study regarding drug consumption using rats. You may have heard of "Rat Park." In one cage, a solitary rat had heroin available to consume as it wished. It consumed plenty and was soon addicted. Later, this same rat was put in a large and well-equipped cage with several other rats. Again, heroin was available. Although addicted, the rat quickly consumed much less of the drug and soon stopped completely. The other rats mostly ignored the heroin. Because of peer pressure, a need to fit in, good examples, nice accommodations and toys, the rat got clean! The researchers believed that group dynamics, the comfort of being with others and a positive environment reduced the rat's desire for drugs. It got its "feel good" from the group! There is also a human example of "Rat Park." During the Vietnam War, many soldiers were receiving Bad Conduct Discharges for using marijuana. Because of this, many others turned to heroin because it was available, cheap, clean and easier to hide. About 20% of the soldiers and sailors that used heroin became addicted. According to a study published by the Archives of General Psychiatry, 95% of these addicts simply stopped after returning home. In the comfort of (mostly) nice people that weren't trying to kill them and a pleasant environment with fun things (Harley-Davidsons, etc.) to play with, they no longer had the need to alter their reality. Welcome home, my brothers!

AA meetings are everywhere. The variety of meetings can be endless. Certainly, large cities have more choices than small towns. Wherever you are, seek out a meeting that best satisfies your needs and become a regular attendee. You may not agree with many sentiments at an AA meeting, but that is not what's important. Attempt to be a friend, regardless of beliefs, and you will find the camaraderie that is important. I attend "normal" AA meetings and a secular meeting that was created two years ago. Even at the secular meeting, I don't agree with everyone regarding beliefs or the lack thereof. Your truth is a very personal thing. Be proud of it and allow all others their own truth. This kindness and respect towards others will reap the warm feeling of community that is essential for the vast majority of us and our sobriety.

In this new century, the internet is providing more information to a wider audience. We are connecting with each other in so many new ways. There are numerous secular websites (aaagnostica.org, secularaa.org) and groups. Social media such as Facebook (Secular AA Coffeeshop, AA Beyond Belief) can be very helpful for connecting with like-minded people. I mention these four things because I am most familiar with them. A quick search of the internet will find many more. If you are having a problem getting a sense of community from AA, reach out to others online. We are beginning to understand that we are not alone in our beliefs (or the lack thereof). There is no reason to hide ourselves. There is no need to pretend you are something you're not in the community of AA. I have found my freedom. I urge you to find yours. Together, we will help each other stay sober. Together, we will find the new life that we all deserve. Together, the rest of our time on this Earth will be amazingly better. Together, we will see that all the ups and downs of life are very normal. Together, we will stay sober long enough to realize "normal" is not good enough! Together, with secular people standing shoulder to shoulder with religious people in support of each other, is the ideal I dream of. That ideal is possible. If I can convince just one other person to join us, we will be closer to achieving it.

A Look Within

Now, what about that second part. Let's explore the AA program. First we need to recognize that the book *Alcoholics Anonymous* was written more than 75 years ago. Many things have changed since 1939. Also, we should recognize that many things are the same. AA's Big Book has an abundance of great ideas and wisdom. But, knowledge and society are advancing at a rapid pace. With the internet available to most people, the world's knowledge is accessible to all. What we can learn is no longer limited to what we are told or taught. With this enhanced ability to enlighten ourselves, we are capable of seeing past some of the biases and fallacies of past teachers. We can develop and expand personal beliefs that are more genuine to who we are. We can understand that truth is not universal or static. My truth is different from your truth. The subject of supernatural beings, and all that encompass it, is increasingly being examined. With all the available scientific knowledge, we are questioning the existence of all gods more and more. This is very disconcerting to people with faith in a god. Therefore, we need to be sensitive to believers. I know. I know. They were rarely, if ever, empathetic to our feelings and beliefs. That doesn't make insensitivity right. Turnaround might be fair play, but it's not appropriate for this spiritual/virtuous life we are seeking. If others choose to be uncaring and unkind, that is their problem. Try not to join them and make a problem for yourself.

Many people are offended by others that hold a contrasting opinion of religious or spiritual matters. Believers in god may be offended by those that don't believe or just question god's existence (and vice versa). Do people have the right to be offended? Of course they do. Everyone has a right to feel any way they wish. I think this is used, much too often, as a defensive mechanism to protect and strengthen your beliefs. It's my opinion that this comes from personal insecurity or fear that your beliefs are not true. If someone is quite confident in their personal beliefs, other's beliefs become irrelevant. Being curious about, and interested in, other's beliefs might become a learning experience.

I am quite content to realize that a lot of my beliefs are not true. Seeking truth is what we should be doing. A person can't be rigid in their beliefs and seek truth at the same time. If you think all of your beliefs are absolutely true, you have no reason to explore new or different ideas anymore. To be close-minded and rigid in your beliefs means you think you know everything. At the very least it means you are comfortable being willfully ignorant.

Perhaps being offended is a defensive posture used because you think you're being attacked on a personal level. If someone is speaking in general terms and you take it personally, that is insecurity and/or fear. Whatever the motivation, being offended is an improper reaction due to a lack of empathy and respect for other's opinions. Blaming others because you are offended is nothing less than excusing your own shortcomings.

Sometimes being offended is a knee-jerk reaction. Take a moment or just take a breath to allow more time between an event and your reaction to it. If you feel a negative reaction within yourself, stop and look for something positive. This takes practice, just like learning to play a musical instrument. Practice long enough and, eventually, you will be making beautiful music!

Personal insults are different. If I say to you, "You're an idiot for believing in God," I deserve to be admonished or worse. Personal insults are wrong. They shouldn't be a part of any type of discourse. If you use personal insults during any conversation or argument, it only means you are being shallow and boorish. "Asshole" might apply, too.

"Beauty is truth, truth beauty,—that is all ye know on earth, and all ye need to know." These are the final lines of the poem *Ode on a Grecian Urn* written by the English poet John Keats in 1819. It sounds wonderful. I believed it for a long time. It sustained my romantic self. Today, I believe beauty is a significant portion of truth, but not "all ye need to know." I want more than a romantic notion. My happiness and serenity cannot be sustained by a single verse. I believe that seeing the beauty in all things is essential for maintaining a positive attitude. Clearing away an abundance of nonsense won't allow us to see all the truths, but it does improve the view. That (improvement) is the objective. How can we accomplish this? How do we go from being drunk and miserable to being sober and happy?

First and foremost we must stop drinking and drugging. The consumption of alcohol and other drugs will forever cloud our thinking and we will constantly be deceiving ourselves. Actually, not drinking and drugging is very simple. You just don't. Don't pick up that drink. Don't pop that pill. Don't snort that line. Don't smoke that joint. Don't pick up that needle. Whatever you are doing to alter your consciousness or shelter yourself from reality, stop it. There! You're done! You fixed that problem! "But, wait," you say, "it can't be that easy." You're right. Most of the time, solutions create more problems. In this case, that oh so very simple solution created a ton of problems! They are what may be called "living problems." How will I ever live without drugs or alcohol? The AA answer is twofold. First, hang around people that are sober for support, inspiration and a sense of community. Secondly, practice virtue and develop serenity. Both of these things make us feel good about ourselves. You have a much better chance for sobriety and happiness when you are likable to yourself and others because you are a nice person. With these positive things in our lives, we will no longer feel a need to alter our reality with alcohol or drugs. Of course, this is so much easier to say than do. That is precisely why we come to AA.

Keep in mind that changing our thinking is not enough. Intellectualizing all this is just the first step. After we change our thinking we must continue in recovery with the changing of our hearts. The "magic" happens when we translate these positive thoughts into good behaviors in our lives. Here is a simple example: Suppose I am acting like a jerk. I will get a negative response from the other person and that will feed my negativity which, in turn, feeds the other person's negativity. All this poor behavior escalates and everyone walks away a loser. Now, imagine that I act kindly, with respect and empathy. I will get a positive response, which makes me feel good because I made the other person feel good. Both of us feel like winners and I like myself because I did a good thing. When I continue to practice virtue, I not only like myself more, but I begin to love myself. It opens my heart to want more and more goodness in my life.

When I start to understand what love is, I can share that love with others. For a long time, I thought love was just a feeling. It was like caring about someone a lot. It is that, but it is so much more! Love is an action, too! Being good, respectable, honorable, charitable, honest, kind, trustworthy, patient, respectful, generous, considerate, helpful and empathetic are all love! Even the Christians agree. The cardinal/theological virtues of the Christian church are faith, hope, charity **_or love_**. Believers and non-believers have common ground!

Love! It's a word that includes all goodness. Its meaning is everything that is good. Love is my higher power. It's not only a power greater than myself, but greater than anything I can imagine! When I open my heart to love, all good and noble things rush in! No amount of booze could possibly be this satisfying and allow me to feel so good!

I know this sounds too wonderful. Certainly, I succeed more on some days than others. That's why it is said that we *practice* virtue. We struggle against our lesser selves all the time. Greed, fear, ignorance, anger, hatred, apathy, selfishness and complacency are a part of each of us. Quite often these things will be in our way. The more I practice virtuous behavior, the more I recognize the negative thoughts I have. At first, it's difficult. The negative thought comes and, before you know it, you followed through and acted poorly.

Don't beat yourself up over it. If you recognize and regret the negative act, you have accomplished something good. Try to be mindful of everything in your life, including your feelings, the people and everything that happens in your day. You are improving if, in retrospect, you can see how you may have acted better. Soon you'll be catching yourself between a bad thought and your corespondent action. In that brief pause between thought and behavior, you'll change course and behave better. Remember how proud you were after that happened. Just like a musical instrument ... we need to practice, practice, practice! With every effort, you will be surprised how much beautiful music you have within you!

I sincerely believe all life is inextricably connected. As humans, we are connected as a species. I think this connection is much deeper than our biological commonality. It's this deep kinship to one another that is something greater than the individual and allows us to go beyond a simple biological bonding. A man in one of my meetings expresses it this way: One person, plus one other person, equals 2.3 people. That is a simple and beautiful answer for a complex idea. Our humanity allows us to love each other. It's easy to express love to someone you actually do love. It takes more effort to express love to a stranger and even more of an endeavor and discipline for someone you don't like. I can't like everyone, but I feel good when I act kindly to someone that I find unpleasant. It is not my job to change the rude, unfriendly or obnoxious person. My only job is to change myself. When I stop judging, criticizing and blaming, I can move forward and embrace acceptance and love. When I act more loving and kindly, others around me act in a more positive manner. Life becomes better and I become happier. With this positive behavior, it is so much easier to maintain my serenity. A singular act of kindness is a wonderful thing! But, keep this in mind. Our goal must be to grow that single act of kindness into a lifestyle. This greater thing is sometimes called god. Sometimes it's called surfing. Call it anything you wish, but one thing is certain. As a human, you are part of it. You'll be so much happier when you choose to be the good and positive part of it.

Running The Gauntlet

AA's program is a great road to a life well lived. Like all roads, it needs to be repaved from time to time. Society is constantly changing. Being flexible and adjusting to these changes is a good thing. If not, we might still be saying words like "thee" and "thou" and wearing powdered wigs. For many people, AA's road, as laid out in the Big Book, is just fine the way it is. And, their comfort with it is okay. It works for them just fine. For a secular person, the AA road is full of potholes. It doesn't matter which of these people you are or what you believe. This is not a them versus us thing. My only intention is to make the AA program palatable for the, seemingly, disenfranchised non-believers among us. I want the AA program to be an all-inclusive thing. I want anyone to have this gift of sobriety available to them "without having to accept someone else's beliefs or having to deny their own."

While reading the book *Alcoholics Anonymous,* a secular person may conclude that it was not written for them. This, I believe, is both true and false. False in that the author's consideration for secularism is minimal. True because it's only temporary. The authors believed everyone will, eventually, become believers in god. Some may disagree because of the "as we understand him" clause, but take a look at that. This is from *Alcoholics Anonymous,* Chapter 5, "How It Works," Step 11: "Sought through prayer and meditation to improve our conscious contact with God *as we understood Him,* praying only for the knowledge of His will for us and the power to carry that out." There is no other option but god. We can understand god as we wish, but we're not even given the opportunity to choose god's gender. Understand him as you wish, but he *WILL* be god and he *WILL* be a male god! No goddesses allowed! That is what I heard when I first read that. And, I believe, I heard exactly what the Christian and patriarchal authors intended. It took me a long time to figure out how I might interpret that so it would be applicable to me.

I believe that the Big Book was not written with respect and acceptance towards secular people, but there is so much wisdom within its pages that it has to be shared with, and more adaptive for, everyone. Unfortunately, translating it into secular thinking is difficult. The requirement for a secular person is to "run the gauntlet" of religiosity while reading it. Either in between the religiosity or because of it, there are many little nuggets of gold to be found. If, while reading, you become dismissive, you might miss the nuggets. It's a struggle, I know. The inclination may be to dismiss the entire work. It will test your patience over and over (which might be a good exercise for your future life of virtue). If you want the program of AA, I believe you should take up this struggle and muster every bit of patience you can. Accept that it will say things in a way that you disagree with. But, if you continue to aim for the larger picture, you will find those things you are looking for.

If you can read *Alcoholics Anonymous* with an open mind, go ahead and do it. You will find your own interpretation of it. That would be wonderful, because we are all individuals with different opinions and understandings. Personally, it took me a long time to get past all the religiosity. I ignored the book for many years. It took me about 10 years to get past what I considered personal insults in the Big Book. It took me over 20 years more to develop the understanding that I have today. No secular member of AA should have to struggle like that. AA's program and fellowship should be readily available to every alcoholic.

As you read *Alcoholics Anonymous,* try to develop a way of reading around the religious content. Try to understand underlying principles and ideas. You do not need to believe in a supernatural being to understand the concepts of spirituality and virtue. This will help you to see the wisdom in this book, instead of being blinded to it. Having empathy will be an important virtue as you read through the text. Empathy is defined as the ability to understand and share the feelings of others. Understanding what the authors mean and the goals they are sharing, as it applies to you, is critical. I might add that understanding and sharing your own feelings will be important commodities, also. Talking to others that accept you as you are will go a long way towards developing an understanding of the AA program. Remember the "fellowship" part of AA. Few, if any, can figure this out on their own. Reliance on others that have travelled this path before you will be invaluable to your continued sobriety.

I have no faith (another intended pun) that Alcoholics Anonymous World Services, Inc. will be changing the Big Book any time soon. AA has been delighted with its Christianity for 80 years, now. AA's refusal to change is its problem. We don't have to let it be our problem. We have the freedom and ability to change it for ourselves.

I thought about whether I should rewrite the entire Big Book or just explain how I modified it for myself. Rewriting it might simplify things, but I don't want to just offer my interpretation. Explaining all of my modifications might be too complicated. I have decided it is best to critique some parts of it and rewrite the first 164 pages which are in the public domain and, therefore, have no copyright protection. In this way, I can offer ideas of how you can modify it for yourself. Also, in this way I can describe why I changed things. Each of us has our own ideas about how AA serves our sobriety. I don't wish to dictate. I only wish to inspire. It is very important for each of us to decide for ourselves what is good or bad, right or wrong and applicable to our sobriety.

You may wish to compare this book to the Big Book. Going back and forth between this book and *Alcoholics Anonymous* may be frustrating or troublesome for some, but I believe the effort will be worthwhile for others. In this way, you are not only reading *Alcoholics Anonymous,* but studying it. We have a lifetime of sobriety ahead of us. Understanding yourself in sobriety is a lifetime endeavor. I suggest you read through my book first. After that, settle in and take months or years to do the comparison. My thoughts and commentaries describe what I believe to be the essence of AA, or things I believe are important or inappropriate for a book that should be inclusive. Take your time. In my opinion, *Alcoholics Anonymous* is not a book that is to be read and forgotten. For some, that is all it's worth. I don't believe it should end up a dust collector on your shelf. That's what happened to my first Big Book. Today, I see it as a textbook. I consider it to be a permanent part of my reading material. I understand that many people will disagree with this. If everyone agreed with me, I would know for sure that something was dreadfully wrong. I didn't write this book thinking I had some secret to a universal truth. That secret isn't within the pages of *Alcoholics Anonymous* either. However, I believe it's a good beginning. I, also, believe that all the magic is within each of us. All texts are no more than guides.

You own your copy of the Big Book. You can alter it as you wish with pen, pencil, felt tip, scissors, glue or fire. Oh … wait … I just heard that as it rolled off my keyboard. I am not an advocate for book burning. I am not an advocate for censorship in any form. I am an advocate for sobriety of any type or methodology. So entertain whatever mood your in. My method was to highlight certain things, cross out other things and make notes in the text and margins. Remember that it's only a guide. As you read the book, make changes as you see fit. Make it work for you. As you grow over the course of time, you might change it over and over again. Your copy might get so marked up that you need to buy another and start over. Do whatever it takes to make it work for you. Your sobriety is far more important than any reverence for the Big Book. Actually, irreverence is one of my favorite things.

So, here we go. Let's start with the "Preface" on page XI. In the second paragraph, the editors describe their great reluctance to make changes in the book. They describe changes as radical. Actually, what is radical is not changing it at all. This is exactly why I'm writing this book. The editors believe AA's success can be attributed to their unflinching narrow-minded view. I'm espousing the idea that AA could be even more successful if it became more open-minded and accepting of all people. I know, I know! Change is hard.

In the "Forward To The First Edition," on page XIV, they use the term "honest desire." Right there is a change. We no longer have to be honest to belong. They go on to say, "We are not allied with any particular faith, sect or denomination, nor do we oppose anyone." The AA-wide use of the Lord's Prayer (a Christian prayer) allies AA with all three of the above. "Nor do we oppose anyone" should mean just that. If those five words need to be explained, you're not as spiritual as you think you are.

As you read through the Big Book, change the word god, supernatural notions or the use of upper-case letters that refer to religious beliefs as you see fit. When I come across the word "god" in the text, it's helpful for me to visualize the lower case. It puts that word in a more appropriate perspective for me. With this method, I can more easily understand that it refers to love, goodness, empathy, virtue, etc. Replace it with whatever works for you. This will help over and over as you read the Big Book.

Many secular people have a problem with the term "spiritual" or "spiritual experience." Many others do not. Always keep in mind that this is your sobriety. Always know that few, if any, of us are capable of realizing all of these ideas on our own. Literature and AA members will contribute to the idea pool. You are the final arbiter of what is right for you.

Always remember that you belong here. Don't let anyone tell

you differently. The dogmatic members of AA have cherry-picked the Big Book so that they may be rigid and discriminatory in their beliefs and behaviors. They want to exclude every alcoholic that not only refuses to believe in their god, but every alcoholic that doesn't hold fast to all their dogmatic views. Dogmatism is a very insidious and unspiritual type of philosophy. Anything that is considered unquestionable should be urgently and thoroughly questioned. Read the previous sentence again.

In the "Forward To The Fourth Edition," on page XXIII, they state, "The stories added to this edition represent a membership whose characteristics of age, gender, race, and culture have widened and have deepened to encompass virtually everyone the first 100 members could have hoped to reach." Apparently, the first 100 members did not hope to reach secular people. Fortunately, they did and we will succeed in sobriety regardless of the difficulties presented to us.

"The Doctor's Opinion," on page XXV is old information, but in so many ways it is still true. A "medical estimate of the plan of recovery" is little more than a quaint idea from this era. On page XXVII, Dr. Silkworth refers to the power of good. That's a nugget. On page XXVIII, there is the first mention of "reliance on things human." That's a reference to all that is not supernatural. We understand that many natural things are not human. We, also, understand that things like fellowship and love are very human. An individual's desire to change, along with our compassion, love, empathy and sharing our experience with the newcomer, is what will work. All that is human power.

Here is something that has always cracked me up! On page XXIX, the good doctor uses the term "psychic change." This is complete nonsense. What's next? Crystal balls and exorcisms? I'm going to give Dr. Silkworth the benefit of the doubt and say he is misusing the term "psychic." Many people, even today, misuse it. In a broad sense, it could be understood to mean something pertaining to the psyche, but it typically, and more properly, means fortune telling, clairvoyance and paranormal things and happenings. These are supernatural things, but the spirit world and religion are two distinctly different studies within that category. Perhaps he means to say psychological. If that is his meaning, I agree with him to an extent. I'm not certain of the "entire" part of it. "A lot" maybe, but "entire"? Maybe we'll just stick with "some" psychological change. Yeah, that works for me.

Dr. Silkworth likes the term "moral psychology," too. Is moral psychology, as used here and earlier, the combination of psychology, philosophy and ethics? He seems to be using this term as something supernatural. I'm certain that Dr. Silkworth was of great benefit to alcoholics and AA in his day. Today, a medical doctor's opinion regarding philosophy, ethics and morality are no more valuable than yours, mine or the plumber's. My apologies to plumbers all over the world if that is taken offensively. I used to be one in my younger days. They have my deepest respect.

On page XXXII, Dr. Silkworth advises us to pray. In many ways, I dislike the notion of prayer. Sometimes it allows the praying person to believe they are doing something helpful, as opposed to getting off their ass and actually being helpful. This is my cynical conclusion. My romantic reasoning wants to see it as a form of hope. It can be an expression of goodwill or the outward manifestation of one's gratitude. Whatever form it may take, being courteous about it is a good exercise in acceptance and understanding of others. Nonetheless, I still won't be saying the "Lord's Prayer" at the end of meetings.

There is much written by and about Bill Wilson. I see him as a person that grew over time. Toward the end of his life, I believe he was much more in favor of accepting and understanding people with differing beliefs. "Bill's Story" is a very early writing. In the middle of page 10, you can see how ignorant he was of atheistic thinking, the origin of the universe and how it works. "I was not an atheist. Few people are, for that means blind faith in…blah, blah, blah." Wilson is being dismissive of atheism and toeing the AA party line. It's not even original. I've heard this argument a million times. This idea makes believers feel good about what we see as their strange proposition of a god in spite of the complete absence of evidence. Herein is the stalemate. Each side thinks the other is preposterous. Leave it alone. It is insignificant. We need to accept others just as we want to be accepted. Actually, Blind Faith is one of my favorite bands so I must be very open-minded, right? Right? Hello? It's okay if you don't understand this joke. I accept your ignorance of '60s classic rock with a side of jazz. See? Acceptance! Easy peasy!

In the middle of page 11, Bill writes, "God had done for him what he could not do for himself. His human will had failed." Try to understand that god's will or your human will are not the only options. Aligning your will to virtue, kindness and love is another wonderful option that works for me. Quite often my human will fails me and I get selfish or self-centered. Sometimes fear creeps into my thinking. Understand that empathy and love are the goals we aspire to. We practice and practice, getting better and better. Realize you will never be perfect. Getting better at being nice is the key to liking/loving yourself and a happier, more fulfilling life without the need to avoid reality by using alcohol and other drugs.

Now that we are past "Bill's Story," I will begin my secular rewriting of the first 164 pages. I have no interest in changing Bill Wilson's story (or anyone else's). So, I guess, all you're going to get is 148 pages. From time to time, I will insert commentary and it will be obvious because it will be labeled and have a different look and feel to it.

So, how shall I approach this section? Well, I've decided to rewrite it as if an agnostic or atheist were writing it. I know this might annoy and antagonize those that may be too close-minded to understand or sympathize with our plight. I'm okay with that. I grew up in the Sixties. It was a time of new thinking, change and turmoil. Protest and defiance were some of the tactics used to influence change. I have learned that, quite often, if you want to make change, sometimes you have to make trouble. If, by doing this, I can influence some to realize how incorrect and inappropriate the book is, it would be wonderful. If not, at least we secular AA members will have something that will help in our quest for sobriety.

Much of this rewriting is word for word as it is in the Big Book. Quite often, the original authors got things right. Sometimes, I changed just a word or two that changes the meaning of a sentence. Other things needed a complete rewrite. I intend to leave references to spirituality because it means so many different things today. I'm certain that some of you wish that I wouldn't. No book can be everything to everyone. I don't wish to exclude anyone. I will open the AA door as wide as possible without closing it for others. Even if you are a radical freethinking intellectual, I'm certain this version will be much more palatable than the original.

I left in the incorrect spelling, grammar and punctuation because I wish to stay as close to the original text as possible. I'm guilty of these same errors. With a bit of luck, the proofreader caught my mistakes. I changed the chapter titles only to distinguish mine from the original text. With the exception of "To Wives*," I think the original titles are fine. Also, I left it as a 1930s' era period piece, but without the misogyny and sexism. Of course, if the text is referring to a specific individual, the gender is left as is. The original text is, at the very least, as sexist as it is religious. I've not heard many women complain about this. Maybe, as a man, I'm not part of those conversations. Maybe it's because women, in general, are kinder than men. Nonetheless, I hope you enjoy this gender-neutral treatment. Here is what I think it might have looked like if it were written in a secular manner with the sole intention of promoting sobriety, and not religious conversion.

Chapter 2
(of the Big Book)

A Solution For All

WE, OF ALCOHOLICS ANONYMOUS, know thousands of men and women who were once just as hopeless as Bill. Nearly all have recovered. They have solved the drink problem.

We are average Americans. All sections of this country and many of its occupations are represented, as well as many political, economic, social, and religious backgrounds. We are people who normally would not mix. But there exists among us a fellowship, a friendliness, and an understanding which is indescribably wonderful. We are like the passengers of a great liner the moment after rescue from shipwreck when camaraderie, joyousness and democracy pervade the vessel from steerage to Captain's table. Unlike the feelings of the ship's passengers, however, our joy in escape from disaster does not subside as we go our individual ways. The feeling of having shared in a common peril is one element in the powerful cement which binds us. But that in itself would never have held us together as we are now joined.

The tremendous fact for every one of us is that we have discovered a common solution. We have a way out on which we can absolutely agree, and upon which we can join in harmonious action. This is the great news this book carries to those who suffer from alcoholism.

An illness of this sort—and we have come to believe it an illness—involves those about us in a way no other human sickness can. If a person has cancer all are sorry for them and no one is angry or hurt. But not so with the alcoholic illness, for with it there goes annihilation of all the things worth while in life. It engulfs all whose lives touch the sufferer's. It brings misunderstanding, fierce resentment, financial insecurity, disgusted friends and employers, warped lives of blameless children, sad spouses, partners and parents—anyone can increase the list.

We hope this volume will inform and comfort those who are, or who may be affected. There are many.

Highly competent psychiatrists who have dealt with us have found it sometimes impossible to persuade an alcoholic to discuss their situation without reserve. Strangely enough, spouses, parents and intimate friends usually find us even more unapproachable than do the psychiatrist and the doctor.

But the ex-problem drinker who has found this solution, who is properly armed with facts about themselves, can generally win the entire confidence of another alcoholic in a few hours. Until such an understanding is reached, little or nothing can be accomplished.

That the person who is making the approach has had the same difficulty, that they obviously know what they are talking about, that their whole deportment shouts at the new prospect that they are a person with a real answer, that they have no attitude of holier than thou, nothing whatever except the sincere desire to be helpful; that there are no fees to pay, no axes to grind, no people to please, no lectures to be endured—these are the conditions we have found most effective. After such an approach many take up their beds and walk again.

None of us makes a sole vocation of this work, nor do we think its effectiveness would be increased if we did. We feel that elimination of our drinking is but a beginning. A much more important demonstration of our principles lies before us in our respective homes, occupations and affairs. All of us spend much of our spare time in the sort of effort which we are going to describe. A few are fortunate enough to be so situated that they can give nearly all their time to the work.

If we keep on the way we are going there is little doubt that much good will result, but the surface of the problem would hardly be scratched. Those of us who live in large cities are overcome by the reflection that close by hundreds are dropping into oblivion every day. Many could recover if they had the opportunity we have enjoyed. How then shall we present that which has been so freely given us?

We have concluded to publish an anonymous volume setting forth the problem as we see it. We shall bring to the task our combined experience and knowledge. This should suggest a useful program for anyone concerned with a drinking problem.

Of necessity there will have to be discussion of matters medical, psychiatric, social, and religious. We are aware that these matters are, from their very nature, controversial. Nothing would please us so much as to write a book which would contain no basis for contention or argument. We shall do our utmost to achieve that ideal. Most of us sense that real tolerance of other people's shortcomings and viewpoints and a respect for their opinions are attitudes which make us more useful to others. Our very lives, as ex-problem drinkers, depend upon our constant thought of others and how we may help meet their needs.

Commentary: The previous paragraph is unchanged from the original text. I have read and reread this paragraph many times. It speaks very well about how AA should be. Unfortunately, these are hollow words. If the authors really meant what they are saying in this paragraph, the book Alcoholics Anonymous would be very different and there would be no need for my book. If everyone applied this paragraph in their daily life, there would be no need for separate agnostic/atheist meetings. There would be no contentious words between believers and non-believers. There would be unquestioning acceptance for every person regardless of beliefs, race, sexual orientation, etc. Because of our fears, these issues remain controversial, but they don't need to be. Respect, acknowledgement and acceptance of all people, as they are, is a very loving, kind and spiritual way of being. Approval of all others is probably too much to ask, but it certainly is a lofty goal that we should aspire to. Unfortunately, in this regard, AA and secular people alike fall short. Familiarity is pleasant. Differences can be uncomfortable. That distressing feeling is fear. We're afraid of not knowing the other person. We're afraid they don't know us. At the least, it can be awkward. The easiest way for me to overcome this fear of the unknown is to be curious. You don't know why someone believes as they do? Ask them. You don't know about gay people? Ask them. You don't know about other cultures? <u>Ask</u>! But then, be prepared to listen. I mean <u>really</u> listen. Get to know others. Learn new ideas and cultures. Experience something distinctive! Don't imprison yourself with only familiar things. I have found other *people and their cultures to be very interesting. The truth is, because of globalization, every part of this world is becoming more diverse. Different cultures are being exposed to each other and, even, blending. Embracing it is the far superior option. Trying to push back against this ever increasing and inevitable reality will only lead to frustration and failure. I try to understand that there are no "others."*

You may already have asked yourself why it is that all of us became so very ill from drinking. Doubtless you are curious to discover how and why, in the face of expert opinion to the contrary, we have recovered from a hopeless condition of mind and body. If you are an alcoholic who wants to get over it, you may already be asking—"What do I have to do?"

It is the purpose of this book to answer such questions specifically. We shall tell you what we have done. Before going into a detailed discussion, it may be well to summarize some points as we see them.

How many times people have said to us: "I can take it or leave it alone. Why can't they?" "Why don't you drink like a lady or quit?" "That fellow can't handle his liquor." "Why don't you try beer and wine?" "Lay off the hard stuff." "Their will power must be weak." "They could stop if they wanted to." "She's such a wonderful woman, I should think he'd stop for her sake." "The doctor told her that if she ever drank again it would kill her, but there she is all lit up again."

Now these are commonplace observations on drinkers which we hear all the time. Back of them is a world of ignorance and misunderstanding. We see that these expressions refer to people whose reactions are very different from ours.

Moderate drinkers have little trouble in giving up liquor entirely if they have good reason for it. They can take it or leave it alone.

Then we have a certain type of hard drinker. They may have the habit badly enough to gradually impair themselves physically and mentally. It may cause them to die a few years before their time. If a sufficiently strong reason—ill health, falling in love, change of environment, or the warning of a doctor—becomes operative, this person can also stop or moderate, although they may find it difficult and troublesome and may even need medical attention.

But what about the real alcoholic? They may start off as a moderate drinker; they may or may not become a continuous hard drinker; but at some stage of their drinking career they begin to lose all control of their liquor consumption, once they start to drink.

Here is the person who has been puzzling you, especially in their lack of control. They do absurd, incredible, tragic things while drinking. They are a real Dr. Jekyll and Mr. Hyde. They are seldom mildly intoxicated. They are always more or less insanely drunk. Their disposition while drinking resembles their normal nature but little. They may be one of the finest people in the world. Yet let them drink for a day, and they frequently become disgustingly, and even dangerously anti-social. They have a positive genius for getting tight at exactly the wrong moment, particularly when some important decision must be made or engagement kept. They are often perfectly sensible and well balanced concerning everything except liquor, but in that respect they are incredibly dishonest and selfish. They often possess special abilities, skills, and aptitudes, and have a promising career ahead of themselves. They use their gifts to build up a bright outlook for their family and themselves, and then pulls the structure down on their head by a senseless series of sprees. They are the person who goes to bed so intoxicated they ought to sleep the clock around. Yet early next morning they search madly for the bottle they misplaced the night before. If they can afford it, they may have liquor concealed all over the house to be certain no one gets their entire supply and throws it down the wastepipe. As matters grow worse, they begin to use a combination of high-powered sedative and liquor to quiet their nerves so they can go to work. Then comes the day when they simply cannot make it and they get drunk all over again. Perhaps they go to a doctor who gives them morphine or some sedative with which to taper off. Then they begin to appear at hospitals and sanitariums.

This is by no means a comprehensive picture of the true alcoholic, as our behavior patterns vary. But this description should identify them roughly.

Why do they behave like this? If hundreds of experiences have shown them that one drink means another debacle with all its attendant suffering and humiliation, why is it they take that one drink? Why can't they stay on the water wagon? What has become of the common sense and will power that they still sometimes display with respect to other matters?

Perhaps there never will be a full answer to these questions. Opinions vary considerably as to why the alcoholic reacts differently from normal people. We are not sure why, once a certain point is reached, little can be done for them. We cannot answer the riddle.

We know that while the alcoholic keeps away from drink, as they may do for months or years, they react much like other people. We are equally positive that once they take any alcohol whatever into their system, something happens, both in the bodily and mental sense, which makes it virtually impossible for them to stop. The experience of any alcoholic will abundantly confirm this.

These observations would be academic and pointless if our friend never took the first drink, thereby setting the terrible cycle in motion. Therefore, the main problem of the alcoholic centers in their mind, rather than in their body. If you ask them why they started on that last bender, the chances are they will offer you any one of a hundred alibis. Sometimes these excuses have a certain plausibility, but none of them really makes sense in the light of the havoc an alcoholic's drinking bout creates. They sound like the philosophy of the person who, having a headache, beats themselves on the head with a hammer so that they can't feel the ache. If you draw this fallacious reasoning to the attention of an alcoholic, they will laugh it off, or become irritated and refuse to talk.

Once in a while they may tell the truth. And the truth, strange to say, is usually that they have no more idea why they took that first drink than you have. Some drinkers have excuses with which they are satisfied part of the time. But in their hearts they really do not know why they do it. Once this malady has a real hold, they are a baffled lot. There is the obsession that somehow, someday, they will beat the game. But they often suspect they are down for the count.

How true this is, few realize. In a vague way their families and friends sense that these drinkers are abnormal, but everybody hopefully awaits the day when the sufferer will rouse themselves from their lethargy and assert their power of will.

The tragic truth is that if the person be a real alcoholic, the happy day may not arrive. They have lost control. At a certain point in the drinking of every alcoholic, they pass into a state where the most powerful desire to stop drinking is of absolutely no avail. This tragic situation has already arrived in practically every case long before it is suspected.

The fact is that most alcoholics, for reasons yet obscure, have lost the power of choice in drink. Our so-called will power becomes practically nonexistent. We are unable, at certain times, to bring into our consciousness with sufficient force the memory of the suffering and humiliation of even a week or a month ago. We are without defense against the first drink.

The almost certain consequences that follow taking even a glass of beer do not crowd into the mind to deter us. If these thoughts occur, they are hazy and readily supplanted with the old threadbare idea that this time we shall handle ourselves like other people. There is a complete failure of the kind of defense that keeps one from putting their hand on a hot stove.

The alcoholic may say to themselves in the most casual way, "It won't burn me this time, so here's how!" Or perhaps they don't think at all. How often have some of us begun to drink in this nonchalant way, and after the third or fourth, pounded on the bar and said to ourselves, "For god's sake, how did I ever get started again?" Only to have that thought supplanted by "Well, I'll stop with the sixth drink." Or "What's the use anyhow?"

When this sort of thinking is fully established in an individual with alcoholic tendencies, they have probably placed themselves beyond help, and unless locked up, may die or go permanently insane. These stark and ugly facts have been confirmed by legions of alcoholics throughout history. But for the grace of our fellowship, there would have been thousands more convincing demonstrations. So many want to stop but cannot.

There is a solution. Almost none of us liked the self-searching, the leveling of our pride, the confession of shortcomings which the process requires for its successful consummation. But we saw that it really worked in others, and we had come to believe in the hopelessness and futility of life as we had been living it. When, therefore, we were approached by those in whom the problem had been solved, there was nothing left for us but to pick up the simple kit of AA tools laid at our feet. We have found much happiness and we have entered into a new state of existence of which we had not even dreamed.

The great fact is just this, and nothing less: That we have had deep and effective spiritual experiences* or life changing ideas which have revolutionized our whole attitude toward life, toward people and toward the universe. The central fact of our lives today is the absolute certainty that our new thinking has entered into our hearts and lives in a way which is indeed incredible. In AA, we have commenced to accomplish those things which we could never do by ourselves.

If you are as seriously alcoholic as we were, we believe there is no middle-of-the-road solution. We were in a position where life was becoming impossible, and if we had passed into the region from which there seems to be no return, we had but two alternatives: One was to go on to the bitter end, blotting out the consciousness of our intolerable situation as best we could; and the other, to accept help. This we did because we honestly wanted to, and were willing to make the effort.

A certain American businessman had ability, good sense, and high character. For years he had floundered from one sanitarium to another. He had consulted the best known American psychiatrists. Then he had gone to Europe, placing himself in the care of a celebrated physician (the psychiatrist, Dr. Jung) who prescribed for him. Though experience had made him skeptical, he finished his treatment with unusual confidence. His physical and mental condition were unusually good. Above all, he believed he had acquired such a profound knowledge of the inner workings of his mind and its hidden springs that relapse was unthinkable. Nevertheless, he was drunk in a short time. More baffling still, he could give himself

*Fully explained—Appendix II

no satisfactory explanation for his fall.

So he returned to this doctor, whom he admired, and asked him point-blank why he could not recover. He wished above all things to regain self-control. He seemed quite rational and well balanced with respect to other problems. Yet he had no control whatever over alcohol. Why was this?

He begged the doctor to tell him the whole truth, and he got it. In the doctor's judgment he was utterly hopeless; he could never regain his position in society and he would have to place himself under lock and key or hire a bodyguard if he expected to live long. That was a great physician's opinion.

But this man still lives, and is a free man. He does not need a bodyguard nor is he confined. He can go anywhere on this earth where other free people may go without disaster, provided he remains willing to maintain a certain simple attitude.

Some of our alcoholic readers may think they can do without a profound change of thinking and the help of others. Let us tell you the rest of the conversation our friend had with his doctor.

Commentary: The original text used the words "spiritual help" instead of "a profound change of thinking and the help of others." Many alcoholics stay sober without "spiritual help." I have no doubt that the author means supernatural help. I, personally, know a few people that stopped without ever setting foot in AA. They decided they were done and that was it. There are many secular people staying sober. There are all sorts of programs and methods that are, quite likely, just as successful as AA. Again, I'll say, "There are as many paths to sobriety as there are people seeking it." There is no one true way. A spiritual experience worked for me and it may work for you, but it is not a prerequisite for sobriety. I will say this though. I believe that seeking and practicing more positive behaviors makes my sobriety a much more pleasant experience. Hence, it is easier for me to stay sober.

The doctor said: "You have the mind of a chronic alcoholic. I have never seen one single case recover, where that state of mind existed to the extent that it does in you." Our friend felt as though the gates of hell had closed on him with a clang.

He said to the doctor, "Is there no exception?"

"Yes," replied the doctor, "there is. Exceptions to cases such as yours have been occurring since early times. Here and there, once in a while, alcoholics have had what are called vital spiritual experiences. To me these occurrences are phenomena. They appear to be in the nature of huge emotional displacements and rearrangements. Ideas, emotions, and attitudes which were once the guiding forces of the lives of these people are suddenly cast to one side, and a completely new set of conceptions and motives begin to dominate them. In fact, I have been trying to produce some such emotional rearrangement within you. With many individuals the methods which I employed are successful, but I have never been successful with an alcoholic of your description."*

---

*For amplification—see Appendix II

Commentary: Here (Appendix II) you will find a good explanation of a "spiritual experience." For many believers it is a supernatural phenomena. For me (and perhaps you) it is a natural phenomena. It's when that cartoonish light bulb above your head appears. It's when you slap your forehead and think, "Wow! That's it!" You get giddy with the realization that, finally, you get it! Sometimes it's not so dramatic. Maybe it's just when you think, "Oh ... okay." What your experience happens to be is irrelevant. Of course, if you would like angels to appear, trumpets blaring and a ray of light to shine on you, I say, "Go for it!" Life is too short to settle.

Upon hearing this, our friend was somewhat relieved, for he reflected that, after all, he was a good church member. This hope, however, was destroyed by the doctor's telling him that while his religious convictions were very good, in his case they did not spell the necessary vital spiritual experience.

Here was the terrible dilemma in which our friend found himself when he had the extraordinary experience, which as we have already told you, made him a free man.

We, in our turn, sought the same escape with all the desperation of a drowning person. What seemed at first a flimsy reed, has proved to be the loving and powerful effects of awakening to goodness. A new life has been given us or, if you prefer, "a design for living" that really works.

The distinguished American psychologist, William James, in his book "Varieties of Religious Experience," indicates a multitude of ways in which people have discovered god. Many of our members seek a new relationship with god, but we have no desire to convince anyone that there is a requirement to have faith in gods. If what we have learned and felt and seen means anything at all, it means that all of us, whatever our race, beliefs, or color are capable of staying sober upon simple and understandable terms as soon as we are willing and honest enough to try. Those having religious affiliations or secular people will find here nothing disturbing to their beliefs. There is no friction among us over such matters.

We think it no concern of ours what religious beliefs, or lack thereof, our members identify themselves with as individuals. This should be an entirely personal affair which each one decides for themselves in the light of past associations, or their present choice. Not all of us join religious bodies, but some of us favor such memberships.

In the following chapter, there appears an explanation of alcoholism, as we understand it, then a chapter addressed to the agnostic. Many who are in this class are among our members. We find such convictions no obstacle to a profound change of thinking or spiritual experience.

Further on, clear-cut directions are given showing how we recovered. These are followed by forty-two personal experiences.

Each individual, in the personal stories, describes in their own language and from their own point of view the way they established their relationship with a power greater than themselves. These give a fair cross section of our membership and a clear-cut idea of what has actually happened in their lives.

Commentary: The personal stories are not a "fair cross section" of the membership. At the very best, it is now a thoroughly outdated cross section. The powers that be need to conduct a much better, open-minded, blinders off examination of AA's membership. Hint: It has grown beyond its previous vast majority of white, male Christians which was the case when the Big Book was written. Yes, they now have stories from other races, women and a Jew. The omission of non-believers is glaring and blatant. AA claims to not be religious, but they believe that goodness can only be experienced through religion.

We hope no one will consider these self-revealing accounts in bad taste. Our hope is that many alcoholic men and women, desperately in need, will see these pages, and we believe that it is only by fully disclosing ourselves and our problems that they will be persuaded to say, "Yes, I am one of them too; I must have this thing."

Chapter 3

More Concerning Alcoholism

MOST OF US have been unwilling to admit we were real alcoholics. No person likes to think they are bodily and mentally different from other people. Therefore, it is not surprising that our drinking careers have been characterized by countless vain attempts to prove we could drink like other people. The idea that somehow, someday they will control and enjoy their drinking is the great obsession of every abnormal drinker. The persistence of this illusion is astonishing. Many pursue it into the gates of insanity or death.

We learned that we had to fully concede to our innermost selves that we were alcoholics. This is the first step in recovery. The delusion that we are like other people, or presently may be, has to be smashed.

We alcoholics are men and women who have lost the ability to control our drinking. We know that no real alcoholic *ever* recovers control. All of us felt at times that we were regaining control, but such intervals—usually brief—were inevitably followed by still less control, which led in time to pitiful and incomprehensible demoralization. We are convinced that alcoholics of our type are in the grip of a progressive illness. Over any considerable period we get worse, never better.

We are like people who have lost their legs; they never grow new ones. Neither does there appear to be any kind of treatment which will make alcoholics of our kind like other people. We have tried every imaginable remedy. In some instances there has been brief recovery, followed always by a still worse relapse. Physicians who are familiar with alcoholism agree there is no such thing as making a normal drinker out of an alcoholic. Science may one day accomplish this, but it hasn't done so yet.

Despite all we can say, many who are real alcoholics are not going to believe they are in that class. By every form of self-deception and experimentation, they will try to prove themselves exceptions to the rule, therefore nonalcoholic. If anyone who is showing inability to control their drinking can do the right-about-face and drink like a lady or gentleman, our hats are off to them. Without question, we have tried hard enough and long enough to drink like other people!

Here are some of the methods we have tried: Drinking beer only, limiting the number of drinks, never drinking alone, never drinking in the morning, drinking only at home, never having it in the house, never drinking during business hours, drinking only at parties, switching from scotch to brandy, drinking only natural wines, agreeing to resign if ever drunk on the job, taking a trip, not taking a trip, swearing off forever (with and without a solemn oath), taking more physical exercise, reading inspirational books, going to health farms and sanitariums, accepting voluntary commitment to asylums—we could increase the list ad infinitum.

We do not like to pronounce any individual as alcoholic, but you can quickly diagnose yourself. Step over to the nearest barroom and try some controlled drinking. Try to drink and stop abruptly. Try it more than once. It will not take long for you to decide, if you are honest with yourself about it. It may be worth a bad case of jitters if you get a full knowledge of your condition.

Commentary: This has nothing to do with secularism. I just wanted to tell you that when I read about trying controlled drinking in my very early sobriety, I decided this was permission to drink. I'm sorry if this breaks your heart, but it's not. Isn't it amazing how well we lie to ourselves? Besides, my controlled drinking experiment failed miserably. By the third day, I was white-knuckling the shit out of it. I think my finger impressions are still in the arms of that chair.

Though there is no way of proving it, we believe that early in our drinking careers most of us could have stopped drinking. But the difficulty is that few alcoholics have enough desire to stop while there is yet time. We have heard of a few instances where people, who showed definite signs of alcoholism, were able to stop for a long period because of an overpowering desire to do so. Here is one.

A man of thirty was doing a great deal of spree drinking. He was very nervous in the morning after these bouts and quieted himself with more liquor. He was ambitious to succeed in business, but saw that he would get nowhere if he drank at all. Once he started, he had no control whatever. He made up his mind that until he had been successful in business and had retired, he would not touch another drop. An exceptional man, he remained bone dry for twenty-five years and retired at the age of fifty-five, after a successful and happy business career. Then he fell victim to a belief which practically every alcoholic has—that his long period of sobriety and self-discipline had qualified him to drink as others do. Out came his carpet slippers and a bottle. In two months he was in a hospital, puzzled and humiliated. He tried to regulate his drinking for a while, making several trips to the hospital meantime. Then, gathering all his forces, he attempted to stop altogether and found he could not. Every means of solving his problem which money could buy was at his disposal. Every attempt failed. Though a robust man at retirement, he went to pieces quickly and was dead within four years.

This case contains a powerful lesson. Most of us have believed that if we remained sober for a long stretch, we could thereafter drink normally. But here is a man who at fifty-five years found he was just where he had left off at thirty. We have seen the truth demonstrated again and again: "Once an alcoholic, always an alcoholic." Commencing to drink after a period of sobriety, we are in a short time as bad as ever. If we are planning to stop drinking, there must be no reservation of any kind, nor any lurking notion that someday we will be immune to alcohol.

Young people may be encouraged by this man's experience to think that they can stop, as he did, on their own will power. We doubt if many of them can do it, because none will really want to stop, and hardly one of them, because of the peculiar mental twist already acquired, will find they can win out. Several of our crowd, people of thirty or less, had been drinking only a few years, but they found themselves as helpless as those who had been drinking twenty years.

To be gravely affected, one does not necessarily have to drink a long time nor take the quantities some of us have. This is particularly true of women or small men. To be sure, this is an issue of metabolism and size not gender. Potential female alcoholics often turn into the real thing and are gone beyond recall in a few years. Certain drinkers, who would be greatly insulted if called alcoholics, are astonished at their inability to stop. We, who are familiar with the symptoms, see large numbers of potential alcoholics among young people everywhere. But try and get them to see it!

As we look back, we feel we had gone on drinking many years beyond the point where we could quit on our will power. If anyone questions whether they have entered this dangerous area, let them try leaving liquor alone for one year. If they are a real alcoholic and very far advanced, there is scant chance of success. In the early days of our drinking we occasionally remained sober for a year or more, becoming serious drinkers again later. Though you may be able to stop for a considerable period, you may yet be a potential alcoholic. We think few, to whom this book will appeal, can stay dry anything like a year. Some will be drunk the day after making their resolutions; most of them within a few weeks.

For those who are unable to drink moderately the question is how to stop altogether. We are assuming, of course, that the reader desires to stop. There was a tremendous urge to cease forever. Yet we found it impossible. This is the baffling feature of alcoholism as we know it—this utter inability to leave it alone, no matter how great the necessity or the wish.

How then shall we help our readers determine, to their own satisfaction, whether they are one of us? The experiment of quitting for a period of time will be helpful, but we think we can render an even greater service to alcoholic sufferers and perhaps to the medical fraternity. So we shall describe some of the mental states that precede a relapse into drinking, for obviously this is the crux of the problem.

What sort of thinking dominates an alcoholic who repeats time after time the desperate experiment of the first drink? Friends who have reasoned with them after a spree which has brought them to the point of divorce or bankruptcy are mystified when they walk directly into a saloon. Why do they? Of what are they thinking?

Our first example is a friend we shall call Jim. This man has a good wife and family. He inherited a lucrative automobile agency. He had a commendable World War record. He is a good salesman. Everybody likes him. He is an intelligent man, normal so far as we can see, except for a nervous disposition. He did no drinking until he was thirty-five. In a few years he became so violent when intoxicated that he had to be committed. On leaving the asylum he came into contact with us.

We told him what we knew of alcoholism and the answer we had found. He made a beginning. His family was re-assembled, and he began to work as a salesman for the business he had lost through drinking. All went well for a time, but he failed to change his thinking. To his consternation, he found himself drunk half a dozen times in rapid succession.

On each of these occasions we worked with him, reviewing carefully what had happened. He agreed he was a real alcoholic and in a serious condition. He knew he faced another trip to the asylum if he kept on. Moreover, he would lose his family for whom he had a deep affection.

Yet he got drunk again. We asked him to tell us exactly how it happened. This is his story: "I came to work on Tuesday morning. I remember I felt irritated that I had to be a salesman for a concern I once owned. I had a few words with the boss, but nothing serious. Then I decided to drive into the country and see one of my prospects for a car. On the way I felt hungry so I stopped at a roadside place where they have a bar. I had no intention of drinking. I just thought I would get a sandwich. I also had the notion that I might find a customer for a car at this place, which was familiar for I had been going to it for years. I had eaten there many times during the months I was sober. I sat down at a table and ordered a sandwich and a glass of milk. Still no thought of drinking. I ordered another sandwich and decided to have another glass of milk.

"Suddenly the thought crossed my mind that if I were to put an ounce of whiskey in my milk it couldn't hurt me on a full stomach. I ordered a whiskey and poured it into the milk. I vaguely sensed I was not being any too smart, but felt reassured as I was taking the whiskey on a full stomach. The experiment went so well that I ordered another whiskey and poured it into more milk. That didn't seem to bother me so I tried another."

Thus started one more journey to the asylum for Jim. Here

was the threat of commitment, the loss of family and position, to say nothing of that intense mental and physical suffering which drinking always caused him. He had much knowledge about himself as an alcoholic. Yet all reasons for not drinking were easily pushed aside in favor of the foolish idea that he could take whiskey if only he mixed it with milk!

Whatever the precise definition of the word may be, we call this plain insanity. How can such a lack of proportion, of the ability to think straight, be called anything else?

You may think this an extreme case. To us it is not far-fetched, for this kind of thinking has been characteristic of every single one of us. We have sometimes reflected more than Jim did upon the consequences. But there was always the curious mental phenomenon that parallel with our sound reasoning there inevitably ran some insanely trivial excuse for taking the first drink. Our sound reasoning failed to hold us in check. The insane idea won out. Next day we would ask ourselves, in all earnestness and sincerity, how it could have happened.

In some circumstances we have gone out deliberately to get drunk, feeling ourselves justified by nervousness, anger, worry, depression, jealousy or the like. But even in this type of beginning we are obliged to admit that our justification for a spree was insanely insufficient in the light of what always happened. We now see that when we began to drink deliberately, instead of casually, there was little serious or effective thought during the period of premeditation of what the terrific consequences might be.

Our behavior is as absurd and incomprehensible with respect to the first drink as that of an individual with a passion, say, for jay-walking. They get a thrill out of skipping in front of fast-moving vehicles. They enjoy themselves for a few years in spite of friendly warnings. Up to this point you would label them as a foolish person having odd ideas of fun. Luck then deserts them and they are slightly injured several times in succession. You would expect them, if they were normal, to cut it out. Presently they are hit again and this time has a fractured skull. Within a week after leaving the hospital a fast-moving trolley car breaks their arm. They tell you they have decided to stop jay-walking for good, but in a few weeks they break both legs.

On through the years this conduct continues, accompanied by their continual promises to be careful or to keep off the streets altogether. Finally, they can no longer work, their spouse gets a divorce and they are held up to ridicule. They try every known means to get the jay-walking idea out of their head. They shut themselves up in an asylum, hoping to mend their ways. But the day they come out they race in front of a fire engine, which breaks their back. Such a person would be crazy, wouldn't they?

You may think our illustration is too ridiculous. But is it? We, who have been through the wringer, have to admit if we substituted alcoholism for jay-walking, the illustration would fit us exactly. However intelligent we may have been in other respects, where alcohol has been involved, we have been strangely insane. It's strong language—but isn't it true?

Some of you are thinking: "Yes, what you tell us is true, but it doesn't fully apply. We admit we have some of these symptoms, but we have not gone to the extremes you people did, nor are we likely to, for we understand ourselves so well after what you have told us that such things cannot happen again. We have not lost everything in life through drinking and we certainly do not intend to. Thanks for the information."

That may be true of certain nonalcoholic people who, though drinking foolishly and heavily at the present time, are able to stop or moderate, because their brains and bodies have not been damaged as ours were. But the actual or potential alcoholic, with hardly an exception, will be absolutely unable to stop drinking on the basis of self-knowledge. This is a point we wish to emphasize and re-emphasize, to smash home upon our alcoholic readers as it has been revealed to us out of bitter experience. Let us take another illustration.

Fred is partner in a well known accounting firm. His income is good, he has a fine home, is happily married and the father of promising children of college age. He has so attractive a personality that he makes friends with everyone. If ever there was a successful businessman, it is Fred. To all appearance he is a stable, well balanced individual. Yet, he is alcoholic. We first saw Fred about a year ago in a hospital where he had gone to recover from a bad case of jitters. It was his first experience of this kind, and he was much ashamed of it. Far from admitting he was an alcoholic, he told himself he came to the hospital to rest his nerves. The doctor intimated strongly that he might be worse than he realized. For a few days he was depressed about his condition. He made up his mind to quit drinking altogether. It never occurred to him that perhaps he could not do so, in spite of his character and standing. Fred would not believe himself an alcoholic. We told him what we knew about alcoholism. He was interested and conceded that he had some of the symptoms, but he was a long way from admitting that he could do nothing about it himself. He was positive that this humiliating experience, plus the knowledge he had acquired, would keep him sober the rest of his life. Self-knowledge would fix it.

We heard no more of Fred for a while. One day we were told that he was back in the hospital. This time he was quite shaky. He soon indicated he was anxious to see us. The story he told is most instructive, for here was a chap absolutely convinced he had to stop drinking, who had no excuse for drinking, who exhibited splendid judgment and determination in all his other concerns, yet was flat on his back nevertheless.

Let him tell you about it: "I was much impressed with what you people said about alcoholism, and I frankly did not believe it would be possible for me to drink again. I rather appreciated your ideas about the subtle insanity which precedes the first drink, but I was confident it could not happen to me after what I had learned. I reasoned I was not so far advanced as most of you, that I had been usually successful in licking my other personal problems, and that I would therefore be successful where you had failed. I felt I had every right to be self-confident, that it would be only a matter of exercising my will power and keeping on guard.

"In this frame of mind, I went about my business and for a time all was well. I had no trouble refusing drinks, and began to wonder if I had not been making too hard work of a simple matter. One day I went to Washington to present some accounting evidence to a government bureau. I had been out of town before during this particular dry spell, so there was nothing new about that. Physically, I felt fine. Neither did I have any pressing problems or worries. My business came off well, I was pleased and knew my partners would be too. It was the end of a perfect day, not a cloud on the horizon.

"I went to my hotel and leisurely dressed for dinner. *As I crossed the threshold of the dining room, the thought came to mind that it would be nice to have a couple of cocktails with dinner. That was all. Nothing more.* I ordered a cocktail and my meal. Then I ordered another cocktail. After dinner I decided to take a walk. When I returned to the hotel it struck me a highball would be fine before going to bed, so I stepped into the bar and had one. I remember having several more that night and plenty next morning. I have a shadowy recollection of being in an airplane bound for New York, and of finding a friendly taxicab driver at the landing field instead of my wife. The driver escorted me about for several days. I know little of where I went or what I said and did. Then came the hospital with unbearable mental and physical suffering.

"As soon as I regained my ability to think, I went carefully over that evening in Washington. *Not only had I been off guard, I had made no fight whatever against the first drink. This time I had not thought of the consequences at all.* I had commenced to drink as carelessly as though the cocktails were ginger ale. I now remembered what my alcoholic friends had told me, how they prophesied that if I had an alcoholic mind, the time and place would come—I would drink again. They had said that though I did raise a defense, it would one day give way before some trivial reason for having a drink. Well, just that did happen and more, for what I had learned of alcoholism did not occur to me at all. I knew from that moment that I had an alcoholic mind. I saw that will power and self-knowledge would not help in those strange mental blank spots. I had never been able to understand people who said that a problem had them hopelessly defeated. I knew then. It was a crushing blow.

"Two of the members of Alcoholics Anonymous came to see me. They grinned, which I didn't like so much, and then asked me if I thought myself alcoholic and if I were really licked this time. I had to concede both propositions. They piled on me heaps of evidence to the effect that an alcoholic mentality, such as I had exhibited in Washington, was a hopeless condition. They cited cases out of their own experience by the dozen. This process snuffed out the last flicker of conviction that I could do the job myself.

"Then they outlined the spiritual answer and program of action which a hundred of them had followed successfully. Though I had been only a nominal churchman, their proposals were not, intellectually, hard to swallow. But the program of action, though entirely sensible, was pretty drastic. It meant I would have to throw several lifelong conceptions out of the window. That was not easy. But the moment I made up my mind to go through with the process, I had the curious feeling that my alcoholic condition was relieved, as in fact it proved to be.

"Quite as important was the discovery that spiritual principles would solve all my problems. I have since been brought into a way of living infinitely more satisfying and, I hope, more useful than the life I lived before. My old manner of life was by no means a bad one, but I would not exchange its best moments for the worst I have now. I would not go back to it even if I could."

Commentary: Fred seems to believe spiritual and religious are interchangeable words. Although many AA members feel the same, it is not true for secular people. Whatever way Fred found sobriety, I am happy for him. There is much truth in Fred's story. Don't get lost in a word. When you read things like "spiritual answer," understand that for some it means a theistic answer. For secular people, it does not. Don't let references like this get your panties bunched up. I feel I should assert, once again, that faith is not a prerequisite for spirituality or having spiritual values. As much as I don't care for the term, "spiritual" is commonly used to mean positive feelings and behaviors. Try to keep in mind that this is 80-year-old thinking the authors are using. Forgive them and put your 21st century spin on it. Over and over, you will see the terms spiritual, spiritual life, spiritual remedy, spiritual answer, etc. Understand that, for secular people, it means virtue. You know, things like love, empathy and kindness. It can mean something different to every person. You get to define it for yourself.

Fred's story speaks for itself. We hope it strikes home to thousands like him. He had felt only the first nip of the wringer. Most alcoholics have to be pretty badly mangled before they really commence to solve their problems.

Many doctors and psychiatrists agree with our conclusions. One of these doctors, staff member of a world-renowned hospital, recently made this statement to some of us: "What you say about the general hopelessness of the average alcoholic's plight is, in my opinion, correct. As to two of you men, whose stories I have heard, there is no doubt in my mind that you were 100% hopeless, apart from divine help. Had you offered yourselves as patients at this hospital, I would not have taken you, if I had been able to avoid it. People like you are too heartbreaking. Though not a religious person, I have profound respect for the spiritual approach in such cases as yours. For most cases, there is virtually no other solution."

Commentary: I am not going to change the doctor's quote. Just keep in mind that divine and spiritual are not the same for secular people. Unless we're talking about Divine, the actor, recording star and international drag icon. I always saw her as wildly spiritual.

Once more: The alcoholic at certain times has no effective mental defense against the first drink. Except in a few rare cases, neither they nor any other human being can provide such a defense. Their defense must come from a power greater than themselves.

Chapter 4

For The Agnostic

Commentary: It's difficult to articulate my feelings about the original Chapter 4. The chapter's deceptive nature is quite repugnant. I could rant and rave, on and on. That might make me feel better, but my feelings are so negative that it would bring me down and you with me. Reading this chapter is the textual equivalent of watching "Reefer Madness." One thing I've come to understand is this: When religious people read this, they believe it is spot on. Their opinion is the result of prejudice towards, and ignorance of, what it is to be agnostic or atheistic. Many of them, truly, believe they have the corner on righteousness all to themselves.

This chapter is, at best, a condescending charade. I find it to be very insulting and incompatible with any secular thinking. By using "We" in the title, it is insinuated that the authors are agnostic. That is so obviously untrue. The author is a Christian trying to save and convert agnostics. This is the part of the Big Book where their blatant proselytizing for god happens. Isn't it odd that they would pretend to be agnostic for god? Attempting a conversion may be understandable, but their duplicity is detestable. I recommend that, if you read the original text, you read it with love in your heart, if possible. You must understand that it is a minefield for resentments.

IN THE PRECEDING chapters you have learned something of alcoholism. It is hoped the authors have made clear the distinction between the alcoholic and non-alcoholic. If, when you honestly want to, you find you cannot quit entirely, or if when drinking, you have little control over the amount you take, you are probably alcoholic. If that be the case, you may be suffering from an illness which only a spiritual or life-changing experience will conquer.

To one who is an atheist or agnostic such an experience is quite possible. To continue as you are would mean disaster. There is no such thing as a hopeless alcoholic. To be doomed to an alcoholic death or to live on a spiritual basis are not always easy alternatives to face.

But it isn't so difficult. About half our original fellowship were of the secular type. At first some of us tried to avoid the issue, hoping against hope we were not true alcoholics. But after a while we had to face the fact that we must find a more loving basis of life—or else. Perhaps it is going to be that way with you. But cheer up, something like half of us were atheists or agnostics. Our experience shows that you need not be disconcerted.

If a mere code of ethics or a better philosophy of life were sufficient to overcome alcoholism, many of us would have recovered long ago. Merely intellectualizing such codes and philosophies is insufficient. The practical application of these principles is the key to success. By realigning your will to be more loving, and practicing this day by day, you will see how much nicer life and sobriety can be.

Lack of power, that was our dilemma. We had to find a power by which we could live, and it had to be a *power greater than ourselves*. This was obvious, but where and how were we to find this power?

Well, that's exactly what this book is about. Its main object is to enable you to find a power greater than yourself which will help solve your problem. That means we have written a book which we believe to be spiritual, virtuous, principled and ethical. And it means, of course, that we are going to talk about god. This should not be a difficulty for agnostics. Accept that most people are religious and find their spirituality through a belief in gods. We should not be prejudiced about how anyone comes to this wonderful way of living. For atheists or agnostics, this power could be as simple as the person you would like to become or the fellowship within AA. Our only concern is the results.

We know how secular people may feel. We have shared an honest doubt and prejudice. Some of us have been violently anti-religious. To others, the word "god" brought up a particular idea with which someone had tried to impress upon them during childhood. We rejected this particular conception because it seemed inadequate. With that rejection we had abandoned the god idea entirely. We were bothered with the thought that dependence upon a supernatural power beyond ourselves was somewhat weak, even cowardly. We looked upon this world of warring individuals, warring theological systems, and inexplicable calamity, with deep skepticism. We looked askance at many individuals who claimed to be godly. How could a supernatural being have anything to do with it all? And who could comprehend a supreme being anyhow? Yet, at other moments, we found ourselves thinking, when enchanted by a starlit night, "The cosmos are so amazing!" There was a feeling of awe and wonder. We held on to that, knowing that we needed no god to be humbled by the immense power and enormous complexity of it all.

Yes, we of agnostic and religious temperaments have had negative thoughts, prejudices and experiences regarding one another. Let us make haste to reassure you. We found that as soon as both were able to lay aside prejudice and express even a willingness to believe in a power greater than ourselves, we commenced to get results, even though it was impossible for any of us, atheist or theist, to fully define or comprehend that power, which could be god, love, fellowship or whatever works for you.

Much to our relief, we discovered we did not need to consider another's conception of a higher power. Our own conception was sufficient to make the approach and to effect a change in our thinking. As soon as we admitted the possible existence of a power greater than ourselves, we began to feel a new sense of power and direction, provided we took other simple steps. We found that these were not difficult terms. To us, the realm of love and selflessness is broad, roomy, all inclusive; never exclusive or forbidding to those who earnestly seek. It is open, we believe, to all persons.

When, therefore, this book uses the term "god" it means your own conception of a higher power. This also applies to other spiritual expressions which you find in this book. Do not let any prejudice you may have against spiritual terms deter you from honestly asking yourself what they mean to you. This was all we needed to commence spiritual growth, to effect our first conscious relation with a higher power as we understood it. Afterward, we found ourselves accepting many things which then seemed entirely out of reach. That was growth, but if we wished to grow we had to begin somewhere. So we used our own conception which may be unlimited.

We needed to ask ourselves but one short question. "Do I now believe, or am I even willing to believe, that there is a power greater than myself?" As soon as a person can say that they do believe, or is willing to believe, we emphatically assure them that they are on their way. It has been repeatedly proven among us that upon this simple cornerstone a wonderfully effective spiritual structure can be built.*

That was great news for us if we thought spiritual principles were only for religious people. When people presented us with spiritual approaches, how frequently did we say, "That's for religious people. It won't work for me because I don't believe in gods." So it was comforting to learn that we could commence without religious beliefs.

Because of a misunderstanding of how spirituality could apply to secular people, we often found ourselves handicapped by obstinacy, sensitiveness, and unreasoning prejudice. Many of us have been so touchy that even casual reference to spiritual things made us bristle with antagonism. This sort of thinking had to be abandoned. Realizing that spirituality means nothing more than a profound new way of thinking about ourselves and others, we found no great difficulty in casting aside such feelings. Faced with alcoholic destruction, we soon became as open minded on these matters as we had tried to be on other questions. In this respect alcohol was a great persuader. It finally beat us into a state of reasonableness. Sometimes this

*Please be sure to read Appendix II on "Spiritual Experience."

was a tedious process; we hope no one else will be prejudiced for as long as some of us were.

The reader may still ask why they should believe in a power greater than themselves. We think there are good reasons. Let us have a look at some of them.

The practical individual of today is a stickler for facts and results. The twentieth century readily accepts scientific theories of all kinds, provided they are firmly grounded in fact. We have numerous theories, for example, about electricity. Everyone believes them without a murmur of doubt. Why this ready acceptance? Simply because, with the scientific method, it is possible to explain what we see, feel, direct, and use, because we have a reasonable assumption as a starting point.

Everybody nowadays, believes in scores of scientific ideas for which there is good evidence, but no perfect visual proof. Quite often, science demonstrates that visual evidence may not tell a complete story. It is being constantly revealed, as we study the material world, that outward appearances are not always inward reality. To illustrate:

The prosaic steel girder is a mass of electrons whirling around each other at incredible speed. These tiny bodies are governed by precise laws, and these laws hold true throughout the material world. Science tells us so. We have no reason to doubt it. Therefore, when the illogical assumption is suggested that underneath the material world and life as we see it, there is an all powerful, guiding, creative intelligence, right there our scientific understanding comes to the surface and we simply reaffirm to ourselves that there is no scientific evidence of it. We read wordy books and indulge in windy arguments, knowing this universe needs no god to explain it. For some who believe in god, these contentions that life originated out of nothing would indicate that life means nothing and proceeds nowhere. We agnostics understand that this explanation of the origins of life "means nothing" of the sort. There is much meaning in life and where it proceeds depends on the behavior we choose today.

We agnostics and atheists chose to believe our human intelligence is never the last word, the alpha and omega, the beginning and end of all. It is merely a tool we use to discover new truths.

We, who have traveled the path of sobriety, beg you to lay aside prejudice, even against organized religion. We have learned that whatever the human frailties of various faiths may be, those faiths have given purpose and direction to millions. All people, believers and non-believers, feel they have a logical idea of what life is all about. Just as we wish to be accepted, we should accept others personal ideas regarding spirituality. All people seek a degree of stability, happiness and usefulness. The path we may choose is not the important thing. The most important thing is our mutual goal of sobriety.

Sometimes we looked at the human defects of people and used their shortcomings as a basis of wholesale condemnation. We talked of intolerance, while we were intolerant ourselves. We missed the reality and the beauty of the forest because we were diverted by the ugliness of some of the trees. It is time to give the loving side of life a fair hearing.

In our personal stories you will find a wide variation in the way each teller approaches and conceives of the power which is greater than themselves. Whether we agree with a particular approach or conception seems to make little difference. Experience has taught us that these are matters about which, for our purpose, we need not be worried. They are questions for each individual to settle for themselves.

On one proposition, however, these men and women are strikingly agreed. Every one of them has gained access to, and believes in, a power greater than themselves. This power has in each case accomplished the seemingly impossible. As a celebrated American figure put it, "Let's look at the record."

Here are thousands of men and women, worldly indeed. They flatly declare that since they have come to believe in a power greater than themselves, to take a certain attitude towards that power, and to do certain simple things, there has been a revolutionary change in their way of living and thinking. In the face of collapse and despair, they found that a new power, peace, happiness, and sense of direction flowed into them. This happened soon after they wholeheartedly met a few simple requirements. Once confused and baffled by the seeming futility of existence, they show the underlying reasons why they were making heavy going of life. Leaving aside the drink question, they tell why living was so unsatisfactory. They show how change came over them. When many hundreds of people are able to say that the consciousness of the presence of a power greater than themselves is today the most important fact of their lives, they present a powerful reason why one should consider a power greater than themselves.

This world of ours has made more progress in the last century than in all the millenniums which went before. Almost everyone knows the reason. Students of ancient history tell us that the intellect of people in those days was equal to the best of today. Yet in ancient times progress was painfully slow. The spirit of modern scientific inquiry, research and invention was almost unknown. People's minds were fettered by superstition, tradition, and all sorts of fixed ideas. Some of the contemporaries of Columbus thought a round earth preposterous. Others came near putting Galileo to death for his astronomical heresies.

Today, it is unnecessary to burden ourselves with fixed ideas like the ancients did. Nonetheless, even in the present century, American newspapers were afraid to print an account of the Wright brothers' first successful flight at Kitty Hawk. Had not all efforts at flight failed before? Did not Professor Langley's flying machine go to the bottom of the Potomac River? Was it not true that the best mathematical minds had proved people could never fly? Had not religious people said god had reserved this privilege to the birds? Only thirty years later the conquest of the air was almost an old story and airplane travel was in full swing.

But in most fields our generation has witnessed complete liberation of our thinking. Show any longshoreman a Sunday supplement describing a proposal to explore the moon by means of a rocket and he will say, "I bet they do it—maybe not so long either." Is not our age characterized by the ease with which we discard old ideas for new, by the complete readiness with which we throw away the theory or gadget which does not work for something new which does?

We had to ask ourselves why we shouldn't apply to our problems this same readiness to change our point of view. We were having trouble with personal relationships, we couldn't control our emotional natures, we were a prey to misery and depression, we couldn't make a living, we had a feeling of uselessness, we were full of fear, we were unhappy, we couldn't seem to be of real help to other people—was not a basic solution of these bedevilments more important than whether we should see newsreels of lunar flight? Of course it was.

When we saw others solve their problems by a simple reliance upon spiritual principles, we had to stop doubting the power of love. Our ideas did not work. But the higher power idea did.

The Wright brothers' faith that they could build a machine which would fly was the mainspring of their accomplishment. Without that, nothing could have happened. We agnostics and atheists were sticking to the idea that self-sufficiency would solve our problems. When others showed us that "group-sufficiency" worked with them, we began to understand why it took **both** of the Wright brothers to succeed in their accomplishment.

Logic is great stuff. We liked it. We still like it. We have the power to reason, to examine the evidence of our senses, and to draw conclusions. That is one of humankind's magnificent attributes. We agnostically inclined would not feel satisfied with a proposal which does not lend itself to reasonable approach and interpretation. Hence we are at pains to tell why we think our ideas are reasonable, why we think it sane and logical, why we say our former thinking was soft and mushy when we tried to figure everything out by ourselves. It takes teamwork and fellowship to come up with all these wonderful new ideas for living a good and sober life.

When we became alcoholics, crushed by a self-imposed crisis we could not postpone or evade, we didn't have to decide the issue of god. There is no need to debate the distinctions of theism and atheism. Whatever your beliefs are regarding this matter, they are sufficient starting points to build a good, strong sobriety.

Arrived at this point, we were squarely confronted with the question of whether the fellowship of Alcoholics Anonymous would work for us. We couldn't duck the issue. Some of us had already walked far over the bridge of reason toward the desired shore of sobriety. The outlines and promises of a new way of living had brought lustre to tired eyes and fresh courage to flagging spirits. Friendly hands had stretched out in welcome. We were grateful that reason had brought us so far. With an open mind, we could easily step ashore. As agnostics, atheists and freethinkers, we lean heavily on reason for support. Combining our ability to reason with the serenity that accompanies love and peace, we receive great support in this last mile.

That was natural, but let us think a little more closely. Without knowing it, we may have been brought to where we stand by a certain kind of faith. For did we not believe in our own reasoning? Did we not have confidence in our ability to think? What was that but a sort of faith in ourselves? Yes, we had been faithful, abjectly faithful to our own ability to reason. So, in a small way, we have the common ground of faith with religious people. We discovered that faith in reason had been involved all the time!

We found that, although we were not worshippers, we were admirers. What a state of mental goose-flesh the word "worship" can bring on! Had we not, variously, admired people, sentiment, things, money, and ourselves? And then, with a better motive, had we not admirably beheld the sunset, the sea, or a flower? Who of us had not loved something or somebody? How much of these feelings, these loves, these admirations, have to do with pure reason? Sometimes, little or nothing, we saw at last. Were not these things the tissue out of which our lives were constructed? Did not these feelings, after all, determine the course of our existence? It was impossible to say we had no capacity for faith, or love, or admiration. In one form or another we had been living by these things often and, sometimes, by little else.

Imagine life without some kind of faith! Were nothing left but pure reason, it wouldn't be much of a life. But we believed in life—of course we did. We can prove life just as we can prove a straight line is the shortest distance between two points. Could we still say the whole thing was nothing but a mass of electrons, created out of nothing, meaning nothing, whirling on to a destiny of nothingness? Of course we could. But, even the electrons themselves seemed more intelligent than that. At least, so the chemist said.

Hence, we see that reason isn't everything. Neither is reason, as some of us use it, entirely dependable. Having said that, there is still no reason (pun intended) to throw it out. Reason emanates from our best minds. The people that proved people could never fly were wrong. At the time, they just didn't understand all the physical science.

Yet we had been seeing another kind of flight, a spiritual liberation in this world, people who rose above their problems. They said love made these things possible, and we only smiled. We had seen spiritual release, but liked to tell ourselves it wasn't true.

Actually we were fooling ourselves, for deep down in every man, woman, and child, is the fundamental idea of love. It may be obscured by calamity, by pomp, by admiration of other things, but in some form or other it is there. For love is a power greater than ourselves, and demonstrations of that power in human lives, are facts as old as human existence itself.

We finally saw that faith in some kind of goodwill was a part of our make-up, just as much as the feelings we have for a friend. Sometimes we had to search fearlessly, but it was there. It was as much a fact as we were. We found this great reality deep down within us. In the last analysis it is only there that love may be found. It was so with us.

We can only clear the ground a bit. If our testimony helps sweep away prejudice, enables you to think honestly, encourages you to search diligently within yourself, then, if you wish, you can join us on this broad journey of sobriety. With this attitude you cannot fail. The consciousness of your beliefs are sure to come to you.

Commentary: The last two pages of the original version of this chapter describe one alcoholic's conversion to a belief in god. I believe it is, completely, irrelevant for secular people. I will not be including it here. I have no desire to change his story, but it has no place in a chapter entitled "We Agnostics." I congratulate him for finding sobriety. We should be grateful for all that find sobriety. Each person must find their own way. Regardless of the fact that a deity doesn't fit into an atheist's life, we should understand and appreciate all paths to sobriety. My big hope is that religious people, as well, will congratulate us and be understanding and grateful for our sobriety.

Chapter 5

How It May Work

Commentary: Before I get started on this chapter, I would like to express my feelings and opinions regarding AA's 12 Steps. Remember that AA has three parts. One is the "fellowship" which allows us a sense of community. Another is the "program" which is a guide for sober living. The 12 Steps are the essence of the program. Service is the third part. It allows us to express our gratitude by giving back to AA and helping others. When I was newly sober and working the 12 Steps, my sponsor insisted that I incorporate each step into my life before I moved on to the next. Each step had to become a normal part of my life. This, I believe, is how I try to become a person of integrity. Each of us has our own path, but this is "How it Worked" for me.

THERE ARE MANY paths to sobriety. We found this path to work for us and we hope it works for you. It will require that you be, completely, honest with yourself. Some people are naturally incapable of grasping and developing a manner of living which demands rigorous honesty. There are such unfortunates. We believe their chances are less than average. There are those, too, who suffer from grave emotional and mental disorders, but many of them do recover if they have the capacity to be honest.

Our stories disclose in a general way what we used to be like, what happened, and what we are like now. If you have decided you want what we have and are willing to go to any length to get it—then you are ready to take certain steps.

At some of these we balked. We thought we could find an easier, softer way. But we could not. With all the earnestness at our command, we beg of you to be fearless and thorough from the very start. Some of us have tried to hold on to our old ideas and the result was nil until we let go absolutely.

Commentary: Here is the now famous "easier, softer way." The beginning of my sobriety was difficult, to say the least. For many years now, I have found sobriety to be the easier, softer way. Being drunk and miserable every day is the most painful and grueling thing I ever did.

Remember that we deal with alcohol—cunning, baffling, powerful! Without help it is too much for us. No one is all powerful—we are here to help. May you find the power of our fellowship now!

Half measures may be enough for some, but most find they avail us nothing. We stood at the turning point. We sought protection and care with complete abandon.

Here are the steps we took, which are suggested as a program of recovery:

1. We admitted we were powerless over alcohol—that our lives had become unmanageable.
2. Came to believe that a power greater than ourselves could restore us to sanity.
3. Made a decision to align our will and our lives with this new-found higher power.
4. Made a searching and fearless inventory of ourselves.

5. Admitted to ourselves and to another human being the exact nature of our wrongs.
6. Were entirely ready to remove all these defects of character.
7. Humbly sought to remove our shortcomings.
8. Made a list of all persons we had harmed, and became willing to make amends to them all.
9. Made direct amends to such people wherever possible, except when to do so would injure them or others.
10. Continued to take personal inventory and when we were wrong promptly admitted it.
11. Sought through open-mindedness, contemplation and meditation to improve our conscious understanding of our higher power, seeking only such knowledge and the willingness to carry that out.
12. Having had a profound awakening as the result of these steps, we tried to carry this message to alcoholics, and to practice these principles in all our affairs.

Many of us exclaimed, "What an order! I can't go through with it." Do not be discouraged. No one among us has been able to maintain anything like perfect adherence to these principles. We are not perfect. The point is, that we are willing to grow along spiritual lines. The principles we have set down are guides to progress. We claim spiritual progress rather than spiritual perfection.

Commentary: I have never heard anyone exclaim, "What an order! I can't go through with it." I left it as is because I think it's funny as hell. At a group I attend, the whole room "exclaims" it when they read "How It Works." At first, I found it annoying. Chanting in unison has never been my thing. Now, I enjoy the humor of it.

Our description of the alcoholic, the chapter to the agnostic, and our personal adventures before and after make clear three pertinent ideas:

(a) That we were alcoholic and could not manage our own lives.
(b) That probably no amount of willpower could have relieved our alcoholism.
(c) That fellowship and a profound change of thinking could and would if it were sought.

Commentary: The original text for (b) was "probably no human power." The authors of the Big Book had no understanding of the probability of human power. I give them credit for even using the word "probably." I'm guessing there was some arm twisting going on regarding this when the book was being written. Nonetheless, it's a wide enough hole for us to drive our secular truck through.

Being convinced, *we were at Step Three*, which is that we decided to align our will and our life with a higher power. Just what do we mean by that, and just what do we do?

The first requirement is that we be convinced that any life run on ego and self-centeredness can hardly be a success. On that basis we are almost always in collision with something or somebody, even though our motives are good. Most people try to live by self-propulsion. Each person is like an actor who wants to run the whole show; is forever trying to arrange the lights, the ballet, the scenery and the rest of the players in their own way. If their arrangements would only stay put, if only people would do as they wished, the show would be great. Everybody, including themselves, would be pleased.

Life would be wonderful. In trying to make these arrangements our actor may sometimes be quite virtuous. They may be kind, considerate, patient, generous; even modest and self-sacrificing. On the other hand, they may be mean, egotistical, selfish and dishonest. But, as with most humans, they are more likely to have varied traits.

Commentary: The original text reads, "any life run on self-will can hardly be a success." I would like to express my thoughts about "will" or "self-will." Everybody has will. Quite often it involves your desire to have life conform to your own ideas. How often have you heard someone in AA say they turned their will over to god, but then took it back? Well, I believe you can't "turn it over" or give it away. If you try, you will soon find it right back were it was because it never left. Much of your will can be taken away if you are a slave or prisoner, but even the slave master or warden can't take it all.

I believe the more suitable approach regarding your will is to align your will with that of the higher power you choose for yourself. My desire ... my will ... today is to align my will with love. I want to embrace love and be more of a loving person. I don't "turn it over" or give it up. I change it. Also, this changing of my will is a life-long process.

The remainder of this chapter is a fair description of applying this new, selfless will in your life. Of course, it encompasses so much more. In sobriety, your conscience begins to work better and better. You will instinctively know what the good thing is. You will easily recognize the loving thing. Remember that whatever you do, whatever decision you have to make, you can ask yourself this simple question: "What is the loving thing?" If you can do this consistently, you will ace the sober life. Others will love you right back! You will feel so good about yourself. You will come to know that no amount of alcohol could come close to making you feel this good. If you understand this, you understand almost all of what the fellowship and program of AA is about.

What usually happens? The show doesn't come off very well. They begin to think life doesn't treat them right. They decide to exert themselves more. They become, on the next occasion, still more demanding or gracious, as the case may be. Still the play does not suit them. Admitting they may be somewhat at fault, they are sure that other people are more to blame. They become angry, indignant, self-pitying. What is their basic trouble? Are they not really a self-seeker even when trying to be kind? Are they not a victim of the delusion that they can wrest satisfaction and happiness out of this world if they only manage well? Is it not evident to all the rest of the players that these are the things they want? And do not their actions make each of them wish to retaliate, snatching all they can get out of the show? Are they not, even in their best moments, a producer of confusion rather than harmony?

Our actor is self-centered—ego-centric, as people like to call it nowadays. They are like the retired businessperson who lolls in the Florida sunshine in the winter complaining of the sad state of the nation; the minister who sighs over the sins of the twentieth century; politicians and reformers who are sure all would be Utopia if the rest of the world would only behave; the outlaw safe cracker who thinks society has wronged them; and the alcoholic who has lost all and is locked up. Whatever our protestations, are not most of us concerned with ourselves, our resentments, or our self-pity?

Selfishness—self-centeredness! That, we think, is the root of our troubles. Driven by a hundred forms of fear, self-delusion, self-seeking, and self-pity, we step on the toes of others and they retaliate. Sometimes they hurt us, seemingly without provocation, but we invariably find that at some time in the past we have made decisions based on self which later placed us in a position to be hurt.

So our troubles, we think, are basically of our own making. They arise out of ourselves, and the alcoholic is an extreme example of self-will run riot, though they usually don't think so. Above everything, we alcoholics must be rid of this selfishness. We must, or it kills us! A higher power makes that possible. And there often seems no way of entirely getting rid of self without this aid. Many of us had ethical and philosophical convictions galore, but we could not live up to them even though we would have liked to. Neither could we reduce our self-centeredness much by wishing or trying on our own power. We had to have the help of a power greater than ourselves.

This is the how and why of it. First of all, we had to quit playing director. It didn't work. Next, we decided that hereafter in this drama of life, our higher power was going to be our director. It is the principal; we are its agents. Most good ideas are simple, and this concept was the keystone of the new and triumphant arch through which we passed to freedom.

When we sincerely took such a position, all sorts of remarkable things followed. We had a new direction. This new power provided what we needed, if we kept closely aligned to it and performed this work well. Established on such a footing we became less and less interested in ourselves, our little plans and designs. More and more we became interested in seeing what we could contribute to life. As we felt new power flow in, as we enjoyed peace of mind, as we discovered we could face life successfully, as we became conscious of this new sense of well being, we began to lose our fear of today, tomorrow or the rest of our lives.

We were now at Step Three. We had rejected our old way of life. Instead, we now strive for personal growth and to be relieved from the bondage of selfishness. We hope that victory over our difficulties will serve as an example to those we might help. We thought well before taking this step making sure we were ready; that we could at last abandon ourselves to our new way of life.

We found it very desirable to take this spiritual step with an understanding person, such as our spouse, best friend, or spiritual adviser. But it is better to do it alone than with one who might misunderstand. The wording was, of course, quite optional so long as we expressed the idea, voicing it without reservation. This was only a beginning, though if honestly and humbly made, an effect, sometimes a very great one, was felt at once.

Next we launched out on a course of vigorous action, the first step of which is a personal housecleaning, which many of us had never attempted. Though our decision was a vital and crucial step, it could have little permanent effect unless at once followed by a strenuous effort to face, and to be rid of, the things in ourselves which had been blocking us. Our liquor was but a symptom. So we had to get down to causes and conditions.

Therefore, we started upon a personal inventory. *This was Step Four.* A business which takes no regular inventory usually goes broke. Taking a commercial inventory is a fact-finding and a fact-facing process. It is an effort to discover the truth about the stock-in-trade. One object is to disclose damaged or unsalable goods, to get rid of them promptly and without regret. If the owner of the business is to be successful, they cannot fool themselves about values.

We did exactly the same thing with our lives. We took stock honestly. First, we searched out the flaws in our make-up which caused our failure. Being convinced that self, manifested in various ways, was what had defeated us, we considered its common manifestations.

Resentment is the "number one" offender. It destroys more alcoholics than anything else. From it stem all forms of spiritual disease, for we have been not only mentally and physically ill, we have been spiritually sick. When the spiritual malady is overcome, we straighten out mentally and physically. In dealing with resentments, we set them on paper. We listed people, institutions or principles with whom we were angry. We asked ourselves why we were angry. In most cases it was found that our self-esteem, our pocketbooks, our ambitions, our personal relationships (including sex) were hurt or threatened. So we were sore. We were "burned up."

Commentary: "Resentment is the 'number one' offender. It destroys more alcoholics than anything else." Can I get an "Amen?" Highlight that sentence. It's not just a nugget. It's worth far more than gold.

On our grudge list we set opposite each name our injuries. Was it our self-esteem, our security, our ambitions, our personal, or sex relations, which had been interfered with?

We were usually as definite as this example:

I'm resentful at:	The Cause	Affects my:
Mr. Brown	His attention to my wife.	Sex relations
	Told my wife of my mistress	Self-esteem (fear)
	Brown may get my job at the office	Security Self-esteem (fear)
Mrs. Jones	She's a nut—she snubbed me. She committed her husband for drinking.	Personal relationship Self-esteem (fear)
	He's my friend. She's a gossip.	
My employer	Unreasonable—Unjust— Overbearing—Threatens to fire me for drinking and padding my expense account.	Self-esteem (fear) Security

| My wife | Misunderstands and nags. Likes Brown. Wants house put in her name | Pride—Personal sex relations— Security (fear) |

We went back through our lives. Nothing counted but thoroughness and honesty. When we were finished we considered it carefully. The first thing apparent was that this world and its people were often quite wrong. To conclude that others were wrong was as far as most of us ever got. The usual outcome was that people continued to wrong us and we stayed sore. Sometimes it was remorse and then we were sore at ourselves. But the more we fought and tried to have our own way, the worse matters got. As in war, the victor only seemed to win. Our moments of triumph were short-lived.

It is plain that a life which includes deep resentment leads only to futility and unhappiness. To the precise extent that we permit these, do we squander the hours that might have been worthwhile. But with the alcoholic, whose hope is the maintenance and growth of a spiritual experience, this business of resentment is infinitely grave. We found that it is fatal. For when harboring such feelings we shut ourselves off from the benefits of goodness. The insanity of alcohol returns and we drink again. And with us, to drink is to die.

If we were to live, we had to be free of anger. The grouch was not for us. This may be the dubious luxury of normal people, but for alcoholics it is poison.

We turned back to the list, for it held the key to the future. We were prepared to look at it from an entirely different angle. We began to see that the world and its people really dominated us. In that state, the wrong-doing of others, fancied or real, had power to actually kill. How could we escape? We saw that these resentments must be mastered, but how? We could not wish them away any more than alcohol.

This was our course: We realized that the people who wronged us were perhaps spiritually sick. Though we did not like their symptoms and the way these disturbed us, they, like ourselves, were sick too. We now wish to show them the same tolerance, pity, and patience that we would cheerfully grant a sick friend. When a person offended we said to ourselves, "This is a sick person. How can I be helpful to them? Instead of being angry, I must remember my newfound level of compassion."

We avoid retaliation or argument. We wouldn't treat sick people that way. If we do, we destroy our chance of being helpful. We cannot be helpful to all people but, because of our new outlook on life, we will know how to take a kindly and tolerant view of each and every one.

Referring to our list again. Putting out of our minds the wrongs others had done, we resolutely looked for our own mistakes. Where had we been selfish, dishonest, self-seeking and frightened? Though a situation had not been entirely our fault, we tried to disregard the other person involved entirely. Where were we to blame? The inventory was ours, not the other person's. When we saw our faults we listed them. We placed them before us in black and white. We admitted our wrongs honestly and were willing to set these matters straight.

Notice that the word "fear" is bracketed alongside the difficulties with Mr. Brown, Mrs. Jones, the employer, and the wife. This short word somehow touches about every aspect of our lives. It was an evil and corroding thread; the fabric of our existence was shot through with it. It set in motion trains of circumstances which brought us misfortune we felt we didn't deserve. But did not we, ourselves, set the ball rolling? Sometimes we think fear ought to be classed with stealing. It seems to cause more trouble.

We reviewed our fears thoroughly. We put them on paper, even though we had no resentment in connection with them. We asked ourselves why we had them. Wasn't it because self-reliance failed us? Self-reliance was good as far as it went, but it didn't go far enough. Some of us once had great self-confidence, but it didn't fully solve the fear problem, or any other. When it made us cocky, it was worse.

Perhaps there is a better way—we think so. For we are now on a different basis; the basis of trusting and relying upon a higher power. We are learning to trust this power greater than ourselves. We are in the world to play the role it guides us towards. Just to the extent that we do as we think it would have us, and humbly rely on it, does it enable us to match calamity with serenity.

We never apologize to anyone for depending upon our higher power. We can laugh at those who think spirituality the way of weakness. Paradoxically, it is the way of strength. The verdict of the ages is that love means courage. All compassionate people have courage. They trust love. We never apologize for doing the loving thing. Instead we let love demonstrate, through us, what it can do. We wish to remove our fear and direct our attention to what our realigned will would have us be. At once, we commence to outgrow fear.

Now about sex. Many of us needed an overhauling there. But above all, we tried to be sensible on this question. It's so easy to get way off the track. Here we find human opinions running to extremes—absurd extremes, perhaps. One set of voices cry that sex is a lust of our lower nature, a base necessity of procreation. Then we have the voices who cry for sex and more sex; who bewail the institution of marriage; who think that most of the troubles of the race are traceable to sex causes. They think we do not have enough of it, or that it isn't the right kind. They see its significance everywhere. One school would allow us no flavor for our fare and the other would have us all on a straight pepper diet. We want to stay out of this controversy. We do not want to be the arbiter of anyone's sex conduct. We all have sex problems. We'd hardly be human if we didn't. What can we do about them?

We reviewed our own conduct over the years past. Where had we been selfish, dishonest, or inconsiderate? Whom had we hurt? Did we unjustifiably arouse jealousy, suspicion or bitterness? Where were we at fault, what should we have done instead? We got this all down on paper and looked at it.

In this way we tried to shape a sane and sound ideal for our future sex life. We subjected each relation to this test—was it selfish or not? We want virtue and love to mold our ideals and help us to live up to them. We remembered always that our sex powers were natural and therefore good, neither to be used lightly or selfishly nor to be despised and loathed.

Whatever our ideal turns out to be, we must be willing to grow toward it. We must be willing to make amends where we have done harm, provided that we do not bring about still more harm in so doing. In other words, we treat sex as we would any other problem. In meditation, we ask ourselves what we should do about each specific matter. The right answer will come, if we want it.

We alone can judge our sex situation. Counsel with persons is often desirable, but we let ourselves, guided by our new principles, be the final judge. We realize that some people are as fanatical about sex as others are loose. We avoid hysterical thinking or advice.

Suppose we fall short of the chosen ideal and stumble? Does this mean we are going to get drunk? Some people tell us so. But this is only a half-truth. It depends on us and on our motives. If we are sorry for what we have done, and have the honest desire for better things, we believe we will be forgiven by those we have harmed and will have learned our lesson. If we are not sorry, and our conduct continues to harm others, we are quite sure to drink. We are not theorizing. These are facts out of our experience.

To sum up about sex: We earnestly hope for the right ideal, for objectivity in each questionable situation, for sanity, and for the strength to do the right thing. If sex is very troublesome, we throw ourselves the harder into helping others. We think of their needs and work for them. This takes us out of ourselves. It quiets the imperious urge, when to yield would mean heartache.

Commentary: Should I point out that the subject of sex is on page 69 of the Big Book? Coincidence? You decide. I, mostly, agree with what the book has to say about sex. Actually, I think the authors should have spent more time and words on the subject. I won't supplement their words because I am not an expert. I guess they weren't, either. I suppose they should be applauded for addressing it at all. I do, however, thoroughly believe we should have a much larger and open conversation about it. Sex is a huge issue for the majority of us. Quite often, the quality and quantity doesn't match our ideals. The angst generated by it is a dangerous thing not only for alcoholics, but society at large. Exercised properly, sex is very beautiful and rewarding. And, especially so if you're sharing it with someone else. Ice cream is my second favorite thing. Combining the two is optional.

If we have been thorough about our personal inventory, we have written down a lot. We have listed and analyzed our resentments. We have begun to comprehend their futility and their fatality. We have commenced to see their terrible destructiveness. We have begun to learn tolerance, patience and good will toward all, even our enemies, for we look on them as sick people. We have listed the people we have hurt by our conduct, and are willing to straighten out the past if we can.

In this book you read again and again that fellowship and a profound change of thinking did for us what we could not do by ourselves. We hope you are convinced now that you can remove whatever has blocked you off from a sober life. If you have already made a decision, and an inventory of your grosser handicaps, you have made a good beginning. That being so you have swallowed and digested some big chunks of truth about yourself.

Commentary: Being willing to give yourself an honest assessment and seeing your real truth is a huge and very important step. You can't fix it if you don't understand how and why it's broken. Realize that this is the hardest part of the program. If you short change this part, it will just take you a lot longer to get where you want to go. Repairing a problem is the beautiful part and that's what comes next. Also, make sure that your personal inventory includes your assets and strengths. Your current and future assets are the tools you will need to help eliminate the liabilities.

Chapter 6

Taking Action

Commentary: This is where all the peace, joy and serenity come into your life. We will never figure it all out, but minimally, we try to do the next right thing. The rewards are far greater than our efforts. The "next right thing" is the best investment we will ever make in ourselves. The title of the chapter pretty much says it all. We can read this book hundreds of times. We can go to Big Book meetings and study it sentence by sentence. We can memorize it. We can quote chapter, verse and page number in meetings. We will sound amazing to other members ... but ... and, this is a big but ... a Bertha Butt (one of the Butt sisters) sized but ... it isn't worth a tinker's dam without the practical application of all the lessons of virtue we learn. Unless we apply all this information into our daily life, it's just so much intellectual masturbation. With the practical application comes all those "promises" on pages 83-84 (of the original text). Actually, the promises were so much more than I ever hoped for when I first got sober. The truth is they fell far short of what became my new life in sobriety.

HAVING MADE our personal inventory, what shall we do about it? We have been trying to get a new attitude, a new understanding of a higher power, and to discover the obstacles in our path. We have admitted certain defects; we have ascertained in a rough way what the trouble is; we have put our finger on the weak items in our personal inventory. Now these are about to be cast out. This requires action on our part, which, when completed, will mean that we have admitted to ourselves, and to another human being, the exact nature of our defects. This brings us to *the Fifth Step* in the program of recovery mentioned in the preceding chapter.

This is perhaps difficult—especially discussing our defects with another person. We think we have done well enough in admitting these things to ourselves. There is doubt about that. In actual practice, we usually find a solitary self-appraisal insufficient. Many of us thought it necessary to go much further. We will be more reconciled to discussing ourselves with another person when we see good reasons why we should do so. The best reason first: If we skip this vital step, we may not overcome drinking. Time after time newcomers have tried to keep to themselves certain facts about their lives. Trying to avoid this humbling experience, they have turned to easier methods. Almost invariably they got drunk. Having persevered with the rest of the program, they wondered why they fell. We think the reason is that they never completed their housecleaning. They took inventory all right, but hung on to some of the worst items in stock. They only *thought* they had lost their egoism and fear; they only *thought* they had humbled themselves. But they had not learned enough of humility, fearlessness and honesty, in the sense we find it necessary, until they told someone else *all* their life story.

More than most people, the alcoholic leads a double life. They are very much the actor. To the outer world they present their stage character. This is the one they like others to see. They want to enjoy a certain reputation, but know in their heart they don't deserve it.

The inconsistency is made worse by the things they do on

their sprees. Coming to their senses, they are revolted at certain episodes they vaguely remember. These memories are a nightmare. They tremble to think someone might have observed them. As fast as they can, they push these memories far inside themselves. They hope they will never see the light of day. They are under constant fear and tension —that makes for more drinking.

Psychologists are inclined to agree with us. We have spent thousands of dollars for examinations. We know but few instances where we have given these doctors a fair break. We have seldom told them the whole truth nor have we followed their advice. Unwilling to be honest with these sympathetic doctors, we were honest with no one else. Small wonder many in the medical profession have a low opinion of alcoholics and their chance for recovery!

We must be entirely honest with somebody if we expect to live long or happily in this world. Rightly and naturally, we think well before we choose the person or persons with whom to take this intimate and confidential step. Those of us belonging to a religious denomination which requires confession must, and of course, will want to go to the properly appointed authority whose duty it is to receive it. Though we have no religious connection, we may still do well to talk with someone ordained by an established religion. We often find such a person quick to see and understand our problem. Of course, we sometimes encounter people who do not understand alcoholics.

If we cannot or would rather not do this, we search our

acquaintance for a close-mouthed, understanding friend. Perhaps our doctor or psychologist will be the person. It may be one of our own family, but we cannot disclose anything to our spouses or our parents which will hurt them and make them unhappy. We have no right to save our own skin at another person's expense. Such parts of our story we tell to someone who will understand, yet be unaffected. The rule is we must be hard on ourself, but always considerate of others.

Notwithstanding the great necessity for discussing ourselves with someone, it may be one is so situated that there is no suitable person available. If that is so, this step may be postponed, only, however, if we hold ourselves in complete readiness to go through with it at the first opportunity. We say this because we are very anxious that we talk to the right person. It is important that they be able to keep a confidence; that they fully understand and approve what we are driving at; that they will not try to change our plan. But we must not use this as a mere excuse to postpone.

When we decide who is to hear our story, we waste no time. We have a written inventory and we are prepared for a long talk. We explain to our partner what we are about to do and why we have to do it. They should realize that we are engaged upon a life-and-death errand. Most people approached in this way will be glad to help; they will be honored by our confidence.

We pocket our pride and go to it, illuminating every twist of character, every dark cranny of the past. Once we have taken this step, withholding nothing, we are delighted. We can look the world in the eye. We can be alone at perfect peace and ease. Our fears fall from us. We begin to have more awareness of our higher power. We may have had certain spiritual beliefs, but now we begin to have a spiritual experience. The feeling that the drink problem has disappeared will often come strongly. We feel we are on a righteous path, walking hand in hand with all that is good in the Universe.

Returning home we find a place where we can be quiet for an hour, carefully reviewing what we have done. We are thankful from the bottom of our heart that we understand our higher power better. Taking this book down from our shelf we turn to the page which contains the twelve steps. Carefully reading the first five proposals we ask if we have omitted anything, for we are building an arch through which we shall walk a free individual at last. Is our work solid so far? Are the stones properly in place? Have we skimped on the cement put into the foundation? Have we tried to make mortar without sand?

If we can answer to our satisfaction, we then look at *Step Six*. We have emphasized willingness as being indispensable. Are we now ready to remove from us all the things which we have admitted are objectionable? Can we rid ourselves of them all — every one? If we still cling to something we will not let go, we dig deeper within ourselves for more willingness.

When ready, we say to ourselves something like this: "I am now willing to recognize and be honest about all of myself, good and bad. I hope that I now can remove from myself every single defect of character which stands in the way of my usefulness to myself and others. I look for strength and inspiration, as I go out from here, to do the loving thing." We have then completed *Step Seven*.

Now we need more action, without which we find "talk is cheap." Let's look at *Steps Eight and Nine*. We have a list of all persons we have harmed and to whom we are willing to make amends. We made it when we took inventory. We subjected ourselves to a drastic self-appraisal. Now we go out to others and repair the damage done in the past. We attempt to sweep away the debris which has accumulated out of our effort to live on a misguided will and run the show ourselves. If we haven't the will to do this, we keep trying until it comes. Remember it was agreed at the beginning *we would go to any lengths for victory over alcohol.*

Probably there are still some misgivings. As we look over the list of business acquaintances and friends we have hurt, we may feel diffident about going to some of them on a spiritual basis. Let us be reassured. To some people we need not, and probably should not emphasize the spiritual feature on our first approach. We might prejudice them. At the moment we are trying to put our lives in order. But this is not an end in itself. Our real purpose is to fit ourselves to be of maximum service to the people about us. It is seldom wise to approach an individual, who still smarts from our injustice to them, and announce that we have found a new way of life in sobriety. In the prize ring, this would be called leading with the chin. Why lay ourselves open to being branded fanatics or bores? We may kill a future opportunity to carry a beneficial message. But the other person is sure to be impressed with a sincere desire to set right the wrong. They are going to be more interested in a demonstration of good will than in our talk of spiritual discoveries.

We don't use this as an excuse for shying away from the subject of our higher power. When it will serve any good purpose, we are willing to announce our convictions with tact and common sense. The question of how to approach the person we hated will arise. It may be they have done us more harm than we have done them and, though we may have acquired a better attitude toward them, we are still not too keen about admitting our faults. Nevertheless, with a person we dislike, we take the bit in our teeth. It is harder to go to an enemy than to a friend, but we find it much more beneficial to us. We go to them in a helpful and forgiving spirit, confessing our former ill feeling and expressing our regret.

Under no condition do we criticize such a person or argue. Simply we tell them that we will never get over drinking until we have done our utmost to straighten out the past. We are there to sweep off our side of the street, realizing that nothing worthwhile can be accomplished until we do so, never trying to tell them what they should do. Their faults are not discussed. We stick to our own. If our manner is calm, frank, and open, we will be gratified with the result.

In nine cases out of ten the unexpected happens. Sometimes the person we are calling upon admits their own fault, so feuds of years' standing melt away in an hour. Rarely do we fail to make satisfactory progress. Our former enemies sometimes praise what we are doing and wish us well. Occasionally, they will offer assistance. It should not matter, however, if someone does throw us out of their office. We have made our demonstration, done our part. It's water over the dam.

Most alcoholics owe money. We do not dodge our creditors. Telling them what we are trying to do, we make no bones about our drinking; they usually know it anyway, whether we think so or not. Nor are we afraid of disclosing our alcoholism on the theory it may cause financial harm. Approached in this way, the most ruthless creditor will sometimes surprise us. Arranging the best deal we can we let these people know we are sorry. Our drinking has made us slow to pay. We must lose our fear of creditors no matter how far we have to go, for we are liable to drink if we are afraid to face them.

Perhaps we have committed a criminal offense which might land us in jail if it were known to the authorities. We may be short in our accounts and unable to make good. We have already admitted this in confidence to another person, but we are sure we would be imprisoned or lose our job if it were known. Maybe it's only a petty offense such as padding the expense account. Most of us have done that sort of thing. Maybe we are divorced, and have remarried but haven't kept up the alimony to number one. They are indignant about it, and have a warrant out for our arrest. That's a common form of trouble too.

Although these reparations take innumerable forms, there are some general principles which we find guiding. Reminding ourselves that we have decided to go to any lengths to find a spiritual experience, we ask that we be given strength and direction to do the right thing, no matter what the personal consequences may be. We may lose our position or reputation or face jail, but we are willing. We have to be. We must not shrink at anything.

Usually, however, other people are involved. Therefore, we are not to be the hasty and foolish martyr who would needlessly sacrifice others to save ourselves from the alcoholic pit. A man we know had remarried. Because of resentment and drinking, he had not paid alimony to his first wife. She was furious. She went to court and got an order for his arrest. He had commenced our way of life, had secured a position, and was getting his head above water. It would have been impressive heroics if he had walked up to the Judge and said, "Here I am."

We thought he ought to be willing to do that if necessary, but if he were in jail he could provide nothing for either family. We suggested he write his first wife admitting his faults and asking forgiveness. He did, and also sent a small amount of money. He told her what he would try to do in the future. He said he was perfectly willing to go to jail if she insisted. Of course she did not, and the whole situation has long since been adjusted.

Before taking drastic action which might implicate other people we secure their consent. If we have obtained permission, have consulted with others, and the drastic step is indicated we must not shrink.

This brings to mind a story about one of our friends. While drinking, he accepted a sum of money from a bitterly-hated business rival, giving him no receipt for it. He subsequently denied having received the money and used the incident as a basis for discrediting the man. He thus used his own wrongdoing as a means of destroying the reputation of another. In fact, his rival was ruined.

He felt that he had done a wrong he could not possibly make right. If he opened that old affair, he was afraid it would destroy the reputation of his partner, disgrace his family and take away his means of livelihood. What right had he to involve those dependent upon him? How could he possibly make a public statement exonerating his rival?

After consulting with his wife and partner he came to the conclusion that it was better to take those risks because he was guilty of such ruinous slander. He saw that he had to place the outcome in the hands of fate or he would soon start drinking again, and all would be lost anyhow. He attended church for the first time in many years. After the sermon, he quietly got up and made an explanation. His action met widespread approval, and today he is one of the most trusted citizens of his town. This all happened years ago.

Commentary: Here is something else that has nothing to do with secularism. Throughout the original text and all the examples of individual alcoholics, the alcoholic is some kind of businessperson with accounts, partners, etc. Bill Wilson, of course, was one of them. There had to be blue-collar types in early AA. I'm not sure what to think of this. It's just something I find odd.

The chances are that we have domestic troubles. Perhaps we are mixed up with others in a fashion we wouldn't care to have advertised. We doubt if, in this respect, alcoholics are fundamentally much worse than other people. But drinking does complicate sex relations in the home. After a few years with an alcoholic, a spouse gets worn out, resentful and uncommunicative. How could they be anything else? We begin to feel lonely, sorry for ourselves. We commence to look around in the night clubs, or their equivalent, for something besides liquor. Perhaps we are having a secret and exciting affair with "the person who understands." In fairness we must say that they may understand, but what are we going to do about a thing like that? A person so involved often feels very remorseful at times, especially if they are married to a loyal and courageous person who has literally gone through hell for them.

Whatever the situation, we usually have to do something about it. If we are sure our spouse does not know, should we tell them? Not always, we think. If they know in a general way that we have been wild, should we tell them in detail? Undoubtedly we should admit our fault. They may insist on knowing all the particulars. They will want to know who the other person is and where they are. We feel we ought to say to them that we have no right to involve another person. We are sorry for what we have done and it shall not be repeated. More than that we cannot do; we have no right to go further. Though there may be justifiable exceptions, and though we wish to lay down no rule of any sort, we have often found this the best course to take.

Our design for living is not a one-way street. It is good for both partners. If we can forget, so can they. It is better, however, that one does not needlessly name a person upon whom the other can vent jealousy.

Perhaps there are some cases where the utmost frankness is demanded. No outsider can appraise such an intimate situation. It may be that both will decide that the way of good sense and loving kindness is to let by-gones be by-gones. Each might contemplate about it, having the other one's happiness uppermost in mind. Keep it always in sight that we are dealing with that most terrible human emotion—jealousy. Good generalship may decide that the problem be attacked on the flank rather than risk a face-to-face combat.

If we have no such complication, there is plenty we should do at home. Sometimes we hear an alcoholic say that the only thing they need to do is to keep sober. Certainly they must keep sober, for there will be no home if they don't. But they are yet a long way from making good to the spouse or parents whom for years they have so shockingly treated. Passing all understanding is the patience parents and spouses have had with alcoholics. Had this not been so, many of us would have no homes today, would perhaps be dead.

The alcoholic is like a tornado roaring their way through the lives of others. Hearts are broken. Sweet relationships are dead. Affections have been uprooted. Selfish and inconsiderate habits have kept the home in turmoil. We feel a person is unthinking when they say that sobriety is enough. They are like the farmer who came up out of the cyclone cellar to find their home ruined. To their spouse, they remarked, "Don't see anything the matter here. Ain't it grand the wind stopped blowin'?"

Yes, there is a long period of reconstruction ahead. We must take the lead. A remorseful mumbling that we are sorry won't fill the bill at all. We ought to sit down with the family and frankly analyze the past as we now see it, being very careful not to criticize them. Their defects may be glaring, but the chances are that our own actions are partly responsible. So we clean house with the family, affirming each morning in meditation that we be patient, tolerant, kindly and loving.

The spiritual life is not a theory. *We have to live it.* Unless one's family expresses a desire to live upon spiritual principles we think we ought not to urge them. We should not talk incessantly to them about spiritual matters. They will change in time. Our behavior will convince them more than our words. We must remember that ten or twenty years of drunkenness would make a skeptic out of anyone.

There may be some wrongs we can never fully right. We don't worry about them if we can honestly say to ourselves that we would right them if we could. Some people cannot be seen— we send them an honest letter. And there may be a valid reason for postponement in some cases. But we don't delay if it can be avoided. We should be sensible, tactful, considerate and humble without being servile or scraping. As sober people we stand on our feet; we don't crawl before anyone.

If we are painstaking about this phase of our development, we will be amazed before we are half way through. We are going to know a new freedom and a new happiness. We will not regret the past nor wish to shut the door on it. We will comprehend the word serenity and we will know peace. No matter how far down the scale we have gone, we will see how our experience can benefit others. That feeling of uselessness and self-pity will disappear. We will lose interest in selfish things and gain interest in others. Self-seeking will slip away. Our whole attitude and outlook upon life will change. Fear of people and of economic insecurity will leave us. We will intuitively know how to handle situations which used to baffle us. We will suddenly realize that we are accomplishing things that we could never do before.

Are these extravagant promises? We think not. They are being fulfilled among us—sometimes quickly, sometimes slowly. They will always materialize if we work for them.

Commentary: Well, here they are! The great and legendary "promises." It's all true. It's a promise for god's sake! No ... really! If you practice a life of virtue and attempt to be a loving person, all this will be yours. In fact, the more devoted you are to this new way of sober living, the more that wonderful things will fill your life. I whole-heartedly believe this simple equation: Love = love in return. It is not karma. It is reality. If you treat someone with kindness they will, usually, react with kindness. If you treat someone negatively they will, usually, react with negativity. And, here's a "truth" that I discovered on this path of love. It is so much easier to be kind and receive kindness. It energizes you as you go about your day. Negativity just sucks the energy right out of you! I came into AA with a ton of substance-induced anxiety so my favorite promise is, "We will comprehend the word serenity and we will know peace." That's the one I wanted. At the time, I thought the promises were just so much hyperbole. But, I really wanted that one. After my sobriety, serenity is the most important thing in my life. I seek it every day. I protect it fiercely. It is how I stay sober and why I stay sober. It is my one asset that allows me to gain all the other assets in my life. I'm a bit OCD, so order is very important to me. Chaos is, to a great degree, a stranger. All this is due to my serenity. It's the foundation of everything good in my life. I say the "Serenity Prayer" over and over. I leave out the word "God." Whenever crap comes into my life, I think about it. I say it to myself. I think about the words and what they mean. I realize how powerful its wisdom is. I don't think of it as a prayer. It's just great advice. It's a major nugget that I can have at my finger tips all day and every day.

This thought brings us to *Step Ten*, which suggests we continue to take personal inventory and continue to set right any new mistakes as we go along. We vigorously commenced this way of living as we cleaned up the past. We have entered the world of kindness and love. Our next function is to grow in understanding and effectiveness. This is not an overnight matter. It should continue for our lifetime. Continue to watch for selfishness, dishonesty, resentment, and fear. When these crop up, we attempt at once to remove them. We discuss them with someone immediately and make amends quickly if we have harmed anyone. Then we resolutely turn our thoughts to someone we can help. Love and tolerance of others is our code.

And we have ceased fighting anything or anyone—even alcohol. For by this time sanity will have returned. We will seldom be interested in liquor. If tempted, we recoil from it as from a hot flame. We react sanely and normally, and we will find that this has happened automatically. We will see that our new attitude toward liquor has been given us without any thought or effort on our part. It just comes! That is the simplicity of it. We are not fighting it, neither are we avoiding temptation. We feel as though we had been placed in a position of neutrality—safe and protected. We have not even sworn off. Instead, the problem has been removed. It does not exist for us. We are neither cocky nor are we afraid. That is our experience. That is how we react so long as we keep in fit spiritual condition.

It is easy to let up on the spiritual program of action and rest on our laurels. We are headed for trouble if we do, for alcohol is a subtle foe. We are not cured of alcoholism. What we really have is a daily reprieve contingent on the maintenance of our spiritual condition. Every day is a day when we must carry the vision of virtue and love into all of our activities. These are thoughts which must go with us constantly. We can exercise our will power along this line all we wish. It is the proper use of the will.

Commentary: The last two sentences of this paragraph are a bit of a nugget. "Will power" means, to me, a kind of forced will. It may be like doing something in spite of the fact that you don't, really, want to do it. In the beginning this is okay. Do whatever it takes. As we grow in sobriety we should realize our will is changing. It is becoming less forced. As we express love and kindness more and more, it becomes easy to see how enjoyable it is. We are aligning our will with love. With practice, this new behavior becomes our nature.

Much has already been said about receiving strength, inspiration, and direction through other AA members, mindfulness and meditation. If we have carefully followed directions, we have begun to sense the flow of love and kindness into us. To some extent we have become conscious of spiritual principles. We have begun to develop this vital sixth sense. But we must go further and that means more action.

Step Eleven suggests open-mindedness, contemplation and meditation. We shouldn't be shy on these matters. Better people than we are using this constantly. It works, if we have the proper attitude and work at it. It would be easy to be vague about this matter. Yet, we believe we can make some definite and valuable suggestions.

*Commentary: In the original text, prayer and meditation is used. Sometimes, I view prayer as a form of hope and best wishes. Those are good things and they will serve you well. Meditation takes many forms and can be very personal. For me, it's those moments when I get into my thoughts. It's a way of getting deep into the moment and connecting with who I am and what I wish to be. I don't spend long times doing it. I just try to have little moments were I'm being mindful of who and where I am and what I'm doing. For me it's a great way to have my mind and my body in the same place. It's being "in the moment." To me it's a better version of AA's slogans "One Day at a Time" and "Live in the Now." Do it any way you wish or don't do it at all. Remember this is **your** sobriety.*

When we retire at night, we constructively review our day. Were we resentful, selfish, dishonest or afraid? Do we owe an apology? Have we kept something to ourselves which should be discussed with another person at once? Were we kind and loving toward all? What could we have done better? Were we thinking of ourselves most of the time? Or were we thinking of what we could do for others, of what we could pack into the stream of life? But we must be careful not to drift into worry, remorse or morbid reflection, for that would diminish our usefulness to others. After making our review we forgive ourselves and think about what corrective measures should be taken.

On awakening let us think about the twenty-four hours ahead. We consider our plans for the day. Before we begin, we affirm that we want our higher power to direct our thinking, especially desiring that it be divorced from self-pity, dishonest or self-seeking motives. Under these conditions we can employ our mental faculties with assurance, knowing we are using our brains for good purpose. Our thought-life will be placed on a much higher plane when our thinking is cleared of wrong motives.

In thinking about our day we may face indecision. We may not be able to determine which course to take. Here we seek inspiration, an intuitive thought or a decision. We relax and take it easy. We don't struggle. We are often surprised how the right answers come after we have tried this for a while. What used to be the hunch or the occasional inspiration gradually becomes a working part of the mind. Being still inexperienced and having just begun this spiritual way of living, it is not probable that we are going to be inspired at all times. We might pay for this presumption in all sorts of absurd actions and ideas. Nevertheless, we find that our thinking will, as time passes, be more and more on the plane of inspiration. We come to rely upon it.

We usually conclude the period of meditation with thoughts of hope and a desire that we learn all through the day what our next step is to be, that we have within us whatever we need to take care of such problems. We hope especially for freedom from selfishness. We may seek for ourselves, however, if others will be helped. We are careful never to wish for our own selfish ends. Many of us have wasted a lot of time doing that and it doesn't work. You can easily see why.

If circumstances warrant, we ask our spouses or friends to join us in morning meditation. We sometimes select and memorize a few set words which emphasize the principles we have been discussing. There are many helpful books also. Also, be quick to see where religious people may be right. You may or may not make use of what they offer.

Commentary: The original text is "Make use of what they offer." I find much in religion to be quite wrong and will not "make use" of that. However, an open mind will discover that some of what it offers is sound advice for spiritual living. Of course, you should decide for yourself what is useful or not. Try to keep in mind the "contempt prior to investigation" idea.

As we go through the day we pause, when agitated or doubtful, and search for the right thought or action. We constantly remind ourselves we are no longer running the show, humbly saying to ourselves many times each day, "Do the next right thing" or asking ourselves, "What is the loving thing?" We are then in much less danger of excitement, fear, anger, worry, self-pity, or foolish decisions. We become much more efficient. We do not tire so easily, for we are not burning up energy foolishly as we did when we were trying to arrange life to suit ourselves.

It works—it really does.

We alcoholics are undisciplined. So we let love and kindness discipline us in the simple way we have just outlined.

But this is not all. There is action and more action. "Talk is cheap." The next chapter is entirely devoted to *Step Twelve*.

Chapter 7

Helping Others

PRACTICAL EXPERIENCE shows that nothing will so much insure immunity from drinking as intensive work with other alcoholics. It works when other activities fail. This is our *twelfth suggestion:* Carry this message to other alcoholics! You can help when no one else can. You can secure their confidence when others fail. Remember they are very ill.

Life will take on new meaning. To watch people recover, to see them help others, to watch loneliness vanish, to see a fellowship grow up about you, to have a host of friends—this is an experience you must not miss. We know you will not want to miss it. Frequent contact with newcomers and with each other is the bright spot of our lives.

Perhaps you are not acquainted with any drinkers who want to recover. You can easily find some by asking a few doctors, ministers, priests or hospitals. They will be only too glad to assist you. Don't be an evangelist or reformer. You will be handicapped if you arouse an understandable prejudice. Ministers and doctors may have some competence and, if so, you can learn from them if you wish, but it happens that because of your own drinking experience you can be uniquely useful to other alcoholics. So cooperate; never criticize. To be helpful is our only aim.

When you discover a prospect for Alcoholics Anonymous, find

out all you can about them. If they do not want to stop drinking, don't waste time trying to persuade them. You may spoil a later opportunity. This advice is given for their family also. They should be patient, realizing they are dealing with a sick person.

If there is any indication that they want to stop, have a good talk with the person most interested in them—usually their spouse. Get an idea of their behavior, their problems, their background, the seriousness of their condition, and their religious leanings. You need this information to put yourself in their place, to see how you would like them to approach you if the tables were turned.

Sometimes it is wise to wait till they go on a binge. The family may object to this, but unless they are in a dangerous physical condition, it is better to risk it. Don't deal with them when they are very drunk, unless they are ugly and the family needs your help. Wait for the end of the spree, or at least for a lucid interval. Then let their family or a friend ask them if they want to quit for good and if they would go to any extreme to do so. If they say yes, then their attention should be drawn to you as a person who has recovered. You should be described to them as one of a fellowship who, as part of their own recovery, try to help others and who will be glad to talk to them if they care to see you.

If they do not want to see you, never force yourself upon them. Neither should the family hysterically plead with them to do anything, nor should they tell them much about you. They should wait for the end of their next drinking bout. You might place this book where they can see it in the interval. Here no specific rule can be given. The family must decide these things. But urge them not to be over-anxious, for that might spoil matters.

Usually the family should not try to tell your story. When possible, avoid meeting a person through their family. Approach through a doctor or an institution is a better bet. If your person needs hospitalization, they should have it, but not forcibly unless they are violent. Let the doctor, if they will, tell them they have something in the way of a solution.

When your person is better, the doctor might suggest a visit from you. Though you have talked with the family, leave them out of the first discussion. Under these conditions your prospect will see they are under no pressure. They will feel they can deal with you without being nagged by their family. Call on them while they are still jittery. They may be more receptive when depressed.

See your person alone, if possible. At first engage in general conversation. After a while, turn the talk to some phase of drinking. Tell them enough about your drinking habits, symptoms, and experiences to encourage them to speak of themselves. If they wish to talk, let them do so. You will thus get a better idea of how you ought to proceed. If they are not communicative, give them a sketch of your drinking career up to the time you quit. But say nothing, for the moment, of how that was accomplished. If they are in a serious mood dwell on the troubles liquor has caused you, being careful not to moralize or lecture. If their mood is light, tell them humorous stories of your escapades. Get them to tell some of theirs.

When they see you know all about the drinking game, commence to describe yourself as an alcoholic. Tell them how baffled you were, how you finally learned that you were sick. Give them an account of the struggles you made to stop. Show them the mental twist which leads to the first drink of a spree. We suggest you do this as we have done it in the chapter on alcoholism. If they are alcoholic, they will understand you at once. They will match your mental inconsistencies with some of their own.

If you are satisfied that they are a real alcoholic, begin to dwell on the hopeless feature of the malady. Show them, from your own experience, how the odd mental condition surrounding that first drink prevents normal functioning of the will power. Don't, at this stage, refer to this book, unless they have seen it and wish to discuss it. And be careful not to brand them as an alcoholic. Let them draw their own conclusion. If they stick to the idea that they can still control their drinking, tell them that possibly they can—if they are not too alcoholic. But insist that if they are severely afflicted, there may be little chance they can recover by themselves.

Continue to speak of alcoholism as an illness, a fatal malady. Talk about the conditions of body and mind which accompany it. Keep their attention focused mainly on your personal experience. Explain that many are doomed who never realize their predicament. Doctors are rightly loath to tell alcoholic patients the whole story unless it will serve some good purpose. But you may talk to them about the hopelessness of alcoholism because you offer a solution. You will soon have your friend admitting they have many, if not all, of the traits of the alcoholic. If their own doctor is willing to tell them that they are alcoholic, so much the better. Even though your protégé may not have entirely admitted their condition, they have become very curious to know how you got well. Let them ask you that question, if they will. *Tell them exactly what happened to you.* Stress the spiritual feature freely. If the person be religious, agnostic or atheist, make it emphatic that *they do not have to agree with your conception of a higher power.* They can choose any conception they like, provided it makes sense to them. *The main thing is that they be willing to believe in a power greater than themselves and that they live by spiritual principles.*

When dealing with any person, you had better use everyday language to describe spiritual principles. There is no use arousing any prejudice they may have, for or against, certain spiritual terms and conceptions about which they may already hold or have rejected. Don't raise such issues, no matter what your own convictions are.

Your prospect may belong to a religious denomination. Their religious education and training may make them feel more knowledgable than you regarding these matters. In that case they are going to wonder how you can add anything to what they already know. But they will be curious to learn why their own convictions have not worked and why yours seem to work so well. They may be an example of the truth that faith alone is insufficient. To be vital, faith in a power greater than yourself must be accompanied by self sacrifice and unselfish, constructive action. Let them see that you are not there to instruct them in religion. Admit that they probably know more about it than you do, but call to their attention the fact that however deep their faith and knowledge, they could not have applied it or they would not drink. Perhaps your story will help them see where they have failed to practice the very precepts they know so well. We represent no religious faith or denomination. We are dealing only with general principles common to most spiritual ways of living.

Outline the program of action, explaining how you made a self-appraisal, how you straightened out your past and why you are now endeavoring to be helpful to them. It is important for them to realize that your attempt to pass this on to them plays a vital part in your own recovery. Actually, they may be helping you more than you are helping them. Make it plain they are under no obligation to you, that you hope only that they will try to help other alcoholics when they escape their own difficulties. Suggest how important it is that they place the welfare of other people ahead of their own. Make it clear that they are not under pressure, that they needn't see you again if they don't want to. You should not be offended if they want to call it off, for they have helped you more than you have helped them. If your talk has been sane, quiet and full of human understanding, you have perhaps made a friend. Maybe you have disturbed them about the question of alcoholism. This is all to the good. The more hopeless they feel, the better. They will be more likely to follow your suggestions.

Your candidate may give reasons why they need not follow all of the program. They may rebel at the thought of a drastic housecleaning which requires discussion with other people. Do not contradict such views. Tell them you once felt as they do, but you doubt whether you would have made much progress had you not taken, at least, some action. On your first visit tell them about the fellowship of Alcoholics Anonymous. If they show interest, lend them your copy of this book.

Unless your friend wants to talk further about themselves, do not wear out your welcome. Give them a chance to think it over. If you do stay, let them steer the conversation in any direction they like. Sometimes a new person is anxious to proceed at once, and you may be tempted to let them do so. This is sometimes a mistake. If they have trouble later, they are likely to say you rushed them. You will be most successful with alcoholics if you do not exhibit any passion for crusade or reform. Never talk down to an alcoholic from any moral or spiritual hilltop; simply lay out the kit of spiritual tools for their inspection. Show them how they worked with you. Offer them friendship and fellowship. Tell them that if they want to get well you will do anything to help.

If they are not interested in your solution, if they expect you to act only as a banker for their financial difficulties or a nurse for their sprees, you may have to drop them until they change their mind. This they may do after they get hurt some more.

If they are sincerely interested and want to see you again, ask them to read this book in the interval. After doing that, they must decide for themselves whether they want to go on. They should not be pushed or prodded by you, their family, or friends. If they are to find sobriety, the desire must come from within.

If they think they can do the job in some other way, or prefer some other spiritual approach, encourage them to follow their own conscience. We have no monopoly on spiritual ideas; we merely have an approach that worked with us. But point out that we alcoholics have much in common and that you would like, in any case, to be friendly. Let it go at that.

Do not be discouraged if your prospect does not respond at once. Search out another alcoholic and try again. You are sure to find someone desperate enough to accept with eagerness what you offer. We find it a waste of time to keep chasing a person who cannot or will not work with you. If you leave such a person alone, they may soon become convinced that they cannot recover by themselves. To spend too much time on any one situation is to deny some other alcoholic an opportunity to live and be happy. One of our fellowship failed entirely with their first half dozen prospects. They often say that if they had continued to work on them, they might have deprived many others, who have since recovered, of their chance.

Suppose now you are making your second visit to a person. They have read this volume and say they are prepared to go through with the Twelve Steps of the program of recovery. Having had the experience yourself, you can give them much practical advice. Let them know you are available if they wish to make a decision and tell their story, but do not insist upon it if they prefer to consult someone else.

They may be broke and homeless. If they are, you might try to help them about getting a job, or give them a little financial assistance. But you should not deprive your family or creditors of money they should have. Perhaps you will want to take the person into your home for a few days. But be sure you use discretion. Be certain they will be welcomed by your family, and that they are not trying to impose upon you for money, connections, or shelter. Permit that and you only harm them. You will be making it possible for them to be insincere. You may be aiding in their destruction rather than their recovery.

Never avoid these responsibilities, but be sure you are doing the right thing if you assume them. Helping others is the foundation stone of your recovery. A kindly act once in a while isn't enough. You have to give of yourself every day, if need be. It may mean the loss of many nights' sleep, great interference with your pleasures, interruptions to your business. It may mean sharing your money and your home, counseling frantic spouses and relatives, innumerable trips to police courts, sanitariums, hospitals, jails and asylums. Your telephone may jangle at any time of the day or night. Your spouse may sometimes say they are neglected. A drunk may smash the furniture in your home, or burn a mattress. You may have to fight with them if they are violent. Sometimes you will have to call a doctor and administer sedatives under their direction. Another time you may have to send for the police or an ambulance. Occasionally you will have to meet such conditions.

We seldom allow an alcoholic to live in our homes for long at a time. It is not good for them, and it sometimes creates serious complications in a family.

Though an alcoholic does not respond, there is no reason why you should neglect their family. You should continue to be friendly to them. The family should be offered your way of life. Should they accept and practice spiritual principles, there is a much better chance that the alcoholic in the family will recover. And even though they continue to drink, the family will find life more bearable.

For the type of alcoholic who is able and willing to get well, little charity, in the ordinary sense of the word, is needed or wanted. The ones who cry for money and shelter before conquering alcohol, are on the wrong track. Yet we do go to great extremes to provide each other with these very things, when such action is warranted. This may seem inconsistent, but we think it is not.

It is not the matter of giving that is in question, but when and how to give. That often makes the difference between failure and success. The minute we put our work on a service plane, the alcoholic commences to rely upon our assistance rather than spiritual principles. They clamor for this or that, claiming they cannot master alcohol until their material needs are cared for. Nonsense. Some of us have taken very hard knocks to learn this truth: Job or no job—spouse or no spouse—we simply do not stop drinking so long as we place dependence upon other people ahead of dependence on our higher power.

Burn the idea into the consciousness of every person that they can get well regardless of anyone. The only condition is that they trust in a higher power of their own understanding and clean house.

Now, the domestic problem: There may be divorce, separation, or just strained relations. When your prospect has made such reparation as they can to their family, and have thoroughly explained to them the new principles by which they are living, they should proceed to put those principles into action at home. That is, if they are lucky enough to have a home. Though their family may be at fault in many respects, they should not be concerned about that. They should concentrate on their own spiritual demonstration. Argument and fault-finding are to be avoided like the plague. In many homes this is a difficult thing to do, but it must be done if any results are to be expected. If persisted in for a few months, the effect on a person's family is sure to be great. The most incompatible people discover they have a basis upon which they can meet. Little by little the family may see their own defects and admit them. These can then be discussed in an atmosphere of helpfulness and friendliness.

After they have seen tangible results, the family will perhaps want to go along. These things will come to pass naturally and in good time provided, however, the alcoholic continues to demonstrate that they can be sober, considerate, and helpful, regardless of what anyone says or does. Of course, we all fall much below this standard many times. But we must try to repair the damage immediately lest we pay the penalty by a spree.

If there be divorce or separation, there should be no undue haste for the couple to get together. The person should be sure of their recovery. The spouse should fully understand the other's new way of life. If their old relationship is to be resumed it must be on a better basis, since the former did not work. This means a new attitude and spirit all around. Sometimes it is to the best interests of all concerned that a couple remain apart. Obviously, no rule can be laid down. Let the alcoholic continue their program day by day. When the time for living together has come, it will be apparent to both parties.

Let no alcoholic say they cannot recover unless they have their family back. This just isn't so. In some cases the spouse will never come back for one reason or another. Remind the prospect that their recovery is not dependent upon people. We believe it is dependent upon fellowship and a profound transformation of our thinking. We have seen people get well whose families have not returned at all. We have seen others slip when the family came back too soon.

Both you and the new person must walk day by day in the path of spiritual progress. If you persist, remarkable things will happen. When we look back, we realize that the things which came to us when we continue to do what is right were better than anything we could have planned. Follow the dictates of a power greater than yourself and you will presently live in a new and wonderful world, no matter what your present- circumstances!

When working with a person and their family, you should take care not to participate in their quarrels. You may spoil your chance of being helpful if you do. But urge upon a person's family that the alcoholic has been a very sick person and should be treated accordingly. You should warn against arousing resentment or jealousy. You should point out that the alcoholic's defects of character are not going to disappear over night. Show them that they have entered upon a period of growth. Ask them to remember, when they are impatient, the wonderful fact of the alcoholic's sobriety.

If you have been successful in solving your own domestic problems, tell the newcomer's family how that was accomplished. In this way you can set them on the right track without becoming critical of them. The story of how you and your spouse settled your difficulties is worth any amount of criticism.

Assuming we are spiritually fit, we can do all sorts of things alcoholics are not supposed to do. People have said we must not go where liquor is served; we must not have it in our homes; we must shun friends who drink; we must avoid moving pictures which show drinking scenes; we must not go into bars; our friends must hide their bottles if we go to their houses; we mustn't think or be reminded about alcohol at all. Our experience shows that this is not necessarily so.

Commentary: The use of the term "moving pictures" is a great example of how old and dated this text is. Of course, the term "movie" is, also, dated and that is still used extensively when describing cinema. Nobody "dials" a phone anymore, either. Maybe I should be ashamed of myself for being negative about these minor and silly things. Perhaps I should recognize them as quaint little things from a bygone era when AA was new and fresh. Recognizing your faults (like this one) is a huge step. Recognizing a problem is, at least, half the battle and, probably, the more difficult part. So, I'm sorry. Please forgive me.

We meet these conditions every day. An alcoholic who cannot meet them, still has an alcoholic mind; there is something the matter with their spiritual status. Their only chance for sobriety would be some place like the Greenland Ice Cap, and even there an Eskimo might turn up with a bottle of scotch and ruin everything! Ask any person who has sent their spouse to distant places on the theory they would escape the alcohol problem.

In our belief any scheme of combating alcoholism which proposes to shield the sick person from temptation is doomed to failure. If the alcoholic tries to shield themselves they may succeed for a time, but they usually wind up with a bigger explosion than ever. We have tried these methods. These attempts to do the impossible have always failed.

So our rule is not to avoid a place where there is drinking, *if we have a legitimate reason for being there.* That includes bars, nightclubs, dances, receptions, weddings, even plain ordinary whoopee parties. To a person who has had experience with an alcoholic, this may seem like tempting fate, but it isn't.

Commentary: Whoopee parties! Go ahead and have a good laugh over that. After you have caught your breath, understand something. Regardless of the humor in this, there is a serious side to it, also. At some point the Big Book may become so outdated, it becomes out of touch and irrelevant. I, sincerely, hope it never comes to that.

You will note that we made an important qualification. Therefore, ask yourself on each occasion, "Have I any good social, business, or personal reason for going to this place? Or am I expecting to steal a little vicarious pleasure from the atmosphere of such places?" If you answer these questions satisfactorily, you need have no apprehension. Go or stay away, whichever seems best. But be sure you are on solid spiritual ground before you start and that your motive in going is thoroughly good. Do not think of what you will get out of the occasion. Think of what you can bring to it. But if you are shaky, you had better work with another alcoholic instead!

Why sit with a long face in places where there is drinking, sighing about the good old days. If it is a happy occasion, try to increase the pleasure of those there; if a business occasion, go and attend to your business enthusiastically. If you are with a person who wants to eat in a bar, by all means go along. Let your friends know they are not to change their habits on your account. At a proper time and place explain to all your friends why alcohol disagrees with you. If you do this thoroughly, few people will ask you to drink. While you were drinking, you were withdrawing from life little by little. Now you are getting back into the social life of this world. Don't start to withdraw again just because your friends drink liquor.

Your job now is to be at the place where you may be of maximum helpfulness to others, so never hesitate to go anywhere if you can be helpful. You should not hesitate to visit the most sordid spot on earth on such an errand. Keep on the firing line of life with these motives and you will be unharmed.

Many of us keep liquor in our homes. We often need it to carry green recruits through a severe hangover. Some of us still serve it to our friends provided they are not alcoholic. But some of us think we should not serve liquor to anyone. We never argue this question. We feel that each family, in the light of their own circumstances, ought to decide for themselves.

We are careful never to show intolerance or hatred of drinking as an institution. Experience shows that such an attitude is not helpful to anyone. Every new alcoholic looks for this spirit among us and is immensely relieved when he finds we are not witch-burners. A spirit of intolerance might repel alcoholics whose lives could have been saved, had it not been for such stupidity. We would not even do the cause of temperate drinking any good, for not one drinker in a thousand likes to be told anything about alcohol by one who hates it.

Some day we hope that Alcoholics Anonymous will help the public to a better realization of the gravity of the alcoholic problem, but we shall be of little use if our attitude is one of bitterness or hostility. Drinkers will not stand for it.

After all, our problems were of our own making. Bottles were only a symbol. Besides, we have stopped fighting anybody or anything. We have to!

Chapter 8

To The Spouse

Commentary: "TO WIVES*" is the title of this chapter in the original text. I would like to point out that asterisk. It references this footnote: "Written in 1939, when there were few women in A.A., this chapter assumes that the alcoholic in the home is likely to be the husband. But many of the suggestions given here may be adapted to help the person who lives with a woman alcoholic—whether she is still drinking or is recovering in A.A." I would like to take a moment to congratulate AA for recognizing this shortcoming in the original text. Unfortunately, they can't bring themselves to change this sexist text for you. Nonetheless, this is proof that AA can and does change when it becomes obvious that change is needed. I applaud them for recognizing that many women are alcoholic. This chapter in the original text is written from the perspective of the spouse of the alcoholic. Was it actually authored by spouses or did the author just pretend to be ... like they did in Chapter 4? The answer is that the author, Bill Wilson, did pretend. "I don't think we should trust a woman to do it right." "Hey ... look ... I'll just pretend to be a wife." "I'm certain nobody will notice." I'm happy that AA has recognized alcoholism among women. I hope I live long enough to see the day that AA recognizes that secular people don't need to be converted or saved by religion to understand spiritual principles. Someday ... maybe ... hopefully ... the powers that be will put an asterisk after the title of the fourth chapter.

WHAT WE HAVE SAID in this book applies to both men and women. In the beginning our fellowship consisted of mostly men, but our activities in behalf of women who drink are on the increase. There is every evidence that women regain their health as readily as men if they try our suggestions.

But for every person who drinks others are involved—the wife or husband who trembles in fear of the next debauch; the mother and father who see their son or daughter wasting away.

Among us are husbands, wives, relatives and friends whose problem has been solved, as well as some who have not yet found a happy solution. We want the spouses of Alcoholics Anonymous to address the spouses of people who drink too much. What they say will apply to nearly everyone bound by ties of blood or affection to an alcoholic.

As spouses of Alcoholics Anonymous, we would like you to feel that we understand as perhaps few can. We want to analyze mistakes we have made. We want to leave you with the feeling that no situation is too difficult and no unhappiness too great to be overcome.

We have traveled a rocky road, there is no mistake about that. We have had long rendezvous with hurt pride, frustration, self-pity, misunderstanding and fear. These are not pleasant companions. We have been driven to maudlin sympathy, to bitter resentment. Some of us veered from extreme to extreme, ever hoping that one day our loved ones would be themselves once more.

Our loyalty and the desire that our husbands and wives hold up their heads and be like other people have begotten all sorts of predicaments. We have been unselfish and self-sacrificing. We have told innumerable lies to protect our pride and our spouses' reputations. We have hoped, we have begged, we have been patient. We have struck out viciously. We have run away. We have been hysterical. We have been terror stricken. We have sought sympathy. We have had retaliatory love affairs.

Our homes have been battlegrounds many an evening. In the morning we have kissed and made up. Our friends have counseled chucking our spouse and we have done so with finality, only to be back in a little while hoping, always hoping. Our spouses have sworn great solemn oaths that they were through drinking forever. We have believed them when no one else could or would. Then, in days, weeks, or months, a fresh outburst.

We seldom had friends at our homes, never knowing how or when the alcoholic of the house would appear. We could make few social engagements. We came to live almost alone. When we were invited out, our spouses sneaked so many drinks that they spoiled the occasion. If, on the other hand, they took nothing, their self-pity made them killjoys.

There was never financial security. Positions were always in jeopardy or gone. An armored car could not have brought the pay envelopes home. The checking account melted like snow in June.

Sometimes there were other men or women. How heartbreaking was this discovery; how cruel to be told they understood our spouse as we did not!

The bill collectors, the sheriffs, the angry taxi drivers, the police, the bums, the friends, and even the lovers they sometimes brought home—our spouses thought we were so inhospitable. "Joykiller, nag, wet blanket"—that's what they said. Next day they would be themselves again and we would forgive and try to forget.

We have tried to hold the love of our children for their alcoholic parent. We have told small tots that father or mother was sick, which was much nearer the truth than we realized. They struck the children, kicked out door panels, smashed treasured crockery, and ripped the keys out of pianos. In the midst of such pandemonium they may have rushed out threatening to live with the other man or woman forever. In desperation, we have even got tight ourselves—the drunk to end all drunks. The unexpected result was that our spouses seemed to like it.

Perhaps at this point we got a divorce and took the children home to father and mother. Then we were severely criticized by our spouse's parents for desertion. Usually we did not leave. We stayed on and on. We finally sought other employment or a second job as destitution faced us and our families.

We began to ask medical advice as the sprees got closer together. The alarming physical and mental symptoms, the deepening pall of remorse, depression and inferiority that settled down on our loved ones—these things terrified and distracted us. As animals on a treadmill, we have patiently and wearily climbed, falling back in exhaustion after each futile effort to reach solid ground. Most of us have entered the final stage with its commitment to health resorts, sanitariums, hospitals, and jails. Sometimes there were screaming delirium and insanity. Death was often near.

Under these conditions we naturally made mistakes. Some of them rose out of ignorance of alcoholism. Sometimes we sensed dimly that we were dealing with sick people. Had we fully understood the nature of the alcoholic illness, we might have behaved differently.

How could someone who loved their spouse and children be so unthinking, so callous, so cruel? There could be no love in such persons, we thought. And just as we were being convinced of their heartlessness, they would surprise us with fresh resolves and new attentions. For a while they would be their old sweet selves, only to dash the new structure of affection to pieces once more. Asked why they commenced to drink again, they would reply with some silly excuse, or none. It was so baffling, so heartbreaking. Could we have been so mistaken in the person we married? When drinking, they were strangers. Sometimes they were so inaccessible that it seemed as though a great wall had been built around them.

And even if they did not love their families, how could they be so blind about themselves? What had become of their judgment, their common sense, their will power? Why could they not see that drink meant ruin to them? Why was it, when these dangers were pointed out that they agreed, and then got drunk again immediately?

These are some of the questions which race through the mind of every person who has an alcoholic spouse. We hope this book has answered some of them. Perhaps your wife or husband has been living in that strange world of alcoholism where everything is distorted and exaggerated. You can see that they really do love you with their better self. Of course, there is such a thing as incompatibility, but in nearly every instance the alcoholic only seems to be unloving and inconsiderate; it is usually because they are warped and sickened that they say and do these appalling things. Today most of our spouses are better partners and parents than ever before.

Try not to condemn the alcoholic no matter what they say or do. They are just another very sick, unreasonable person. Treat them, when you can, as though they had pneumonia. When they anger you, remember that they are very ill.

There is an important exception to the foregoing. We realize some people are thoroughly bad-intentioned, that no amount of patience will make any difference. An alcoholic of this temperament may be quick to use this chapter as a club over your head. Don't let them get away with it. If you are positive they are one of this type you may feel you had better leave. Is it right to let them ruin your life and the lives of your children? Especially when they have before them a way to stop their drinking and abuse if they really want to pay the price.

The problem with which you struggle usually falls within one of four categories:

One: Your spouse may be only a heavy drinker. Their drinking may be constant or it may be heavy only on certain occasions. Perhaps they spend too much money for liquor. It may be slowing them up mentally and physically, but they do not see it. Sometimes they are a source of embarrassment to you and their friends. They are positive they can handle their liquor, that it does them no harm, that drinking is necessary in their business. They would probably be insulted if they were called an alcoholic. This world is full of people like them. Some will moderate or stop altogether, and some will not. Of those who keep on, a good number will become true alcoholics after a while.

Two: Your spouse is showing lack of control, for they are unable to stay on the water wagon even when they want to. They often get entirely out of hand when drinking. They admit this is true, but are positive that they will do better. They have begun to try, with or without your cooperation, various means of moderating or staying dry. Maybe they are beginning to lose their friends. Their work life may suffer somewhat. They are worried at times, and are becoming aware that they cannot drink like other people. They sometimes drink in the morning and through the day also, to hold their nervousness in check. They are remorseful after serious drinking bouts and tell you they want to stop. But when they get over the spree, they begin to think once more how they can drink moderately next time. We think this person is in danger. These are the earmarks of a real alcoholic. Perhaps they can still tend to business fairly well. They have by no means ruined everything. As we say among ourselves, *"They want to want to stop."*

Three: This spouse has gone much further than spouse number two. Though once like number two they became worse. Their friends have slipped away, their home is a near-wreck and they cannot hold a position. Maybe the doctor has been called in, and the weary round of sanitariums and hospitals has begun. They admit they cannot drink like other people, but do not see why. They cling to the notion that they will yet find a way to do so. They may have come to the point where they desperately want to stop but cannot. Their case presents additional questions which we shall try to answer for you. You can be quite hopeful of a situation like this.

Four: You may have a spouse of whom you completely despair. They have been placed in one institution after another. They are violent, or appear definitely insane when drunk. Sometimes they drink on the way home from the hospital. Perhaps they have had delirium tremens. Doctors may shake their heads and advise you to have them committed. Maybe you have already been obliged to put them away. This picture may not be as dark as it looks. Many of our partners were just as far gone. Yet they got well.

Let's now go back to spouse number one. Oddly enough, they are often difficult to deal with. They enjoy drinking. It stirs their imagination. Their friends feel closer over a highball. Perhaps you enjoy drinking with them yourself when they don't go too far. You have passed happy evenings together chatting and drinking before your fire. Perhaps you both like parties which would be dull without liquor. We have enjoyed such evenings ourselves; we had a good time. We know all about liquor as a social lubricant. Some, but not all of us, think it has its advantages when reasonably used.

The first principle of success is that you should never be angry. Even though your spouse becomes unbearable and you have to leave them temporarily, you should, if you can, go without rancor. Patience and good temper are most necessary.

Our next thought is that you should never tell them what they must do about their drinking. If they get the idea that you are a nag or a killjoy, your chance of accomplishing anything useful may be zero. They will use that as an excuse to drink more. They will tell you they are misunderstood. This may lead to lonely evenings for you. They may seek someone else to console them—perhaps a new lover.

Be determined that your partner's drinking is not going to spoil your relations with your children or your friends. They need your companionship and your help. It is possible to have a full and useful life, though your husband or wife continues to drink. We know men and women who are unafraid, even happy under these conditions. Do not set your heart on reforming your partner. You may be unable to do so, no matter how hard you try.

We know these suggestions are sometimes difficult to follow, but you will save many a heartbreak if you can succeed in observing them. Your spouse may come to appreciate your reasonableness and patience. This may lay the groundwork for a friendly talk about their alcoholic problem. Try to have them bring up the subject themselves. Be sure you are not critical during such a discussion. Attempt instead, to put yourself in their place. Let them see that you want to be helpful rather than critical.

When a discussion does arise, you might suggest they read this book or at least the chapter on alcoholism. Tell them you have been worried, though perhaps needlessly. You think they ought to know the subject better, as everyone should have a clear understanding of the risk they take if they drink too much. Show them you have confidence in their power to stop or moderate. Say you do not want to be a wet blanket; that you only want them to take care of their health. Thus you may succeed in interesting them in alcoholism.

They probably have several alcoholics among their own acquaintances. You might suggest that you both take an interest in them. Drinkers like to help other drinkers. Your spouse may be willing to talk to one of them.

If this kind of approach does not catch your spouse's interest, it may be best to drop the subject, but after a friendly talk they will usually revive the topic themselves. This may take patient waiting, but it will be worth it. Meanwhile you might try to help the spouse of another serious drinker. If you act upon these principles, your spouse may stop or moderate.

Suppose, however, that your husband or wife fits the description of number two. The same principles which apply to spouse number one should be practiced. But after the next binge, ask them if they would really like to get over drinking for good. Do not ask that they do it for you or anyone else. Just would they like to?

The chances are they would. Show them your copy of this book and tell them what you have found out about alcoholism. Show them that as alcoholics, the writers of the book understand. Tell them some of the interesting stories you have read. If you think they will be shy of a spiritual remedy, ask them to look at the chapter on alcoholism. Then perhaps they will be interested enough to continue.

If they are enthusiastic your cooperation will mean a great deal. If they are lukewarm or think they are not an alcoholic, we suggest you leave them alone. Avoid urging them to follow our program. The seed has been planted in their mind. They know that thousands of people, much like themselves, have recovered. But don't remind them of this after they have been drinking, for they may be angry. Sooner or later, you are likely to find them reading the book once more. Wait until repeated stumbling convinces them they must act, for the more you hurry them the longer their recovery may be delayed.

If you have a number three spouse, you may be in luck. Being certain they want to stop, you can go to them with this volume as joyfully as though you had struck oil. They may not share your enthusiasm, but they are practically sure to read the book and they may go for the program at once. If they do not, you will probably not have long to wait. Again, you should not crowd them. Let them decide for themselves. Cheerfully see them through more sprees. Talk about their condition or this book only when they raise the issue. In some cases it may be better to let someone outside the family present the book. They can urge action without arousing hostility. If your partner is otherwise a normal individual, your chances are good at this stage.

You would suppose that people in the fourth classification would be quite hopeless, but that is not so. Many of Alcoholics Anonymous were like that. Everybody had given them up. Defeat seemed certain. Yet often such people had spectacular and powerful recoveries.

There are exceptions. Some have been so impaired by alcohol that they cannot stop. Sometimes there are cases where alcoholism is complicated by other disorders. A good doctor or psychiatrist can tell you whether these complications are serious. In any event, try to have your spouse read this book. Their reaction may be one of enthusiasm. If they are already committed to an institution, but can convince you and your doctor that they mean business, give them a chance to try our method, unless the doctor thinks their mental condition too abnormal or dangerous. We make this recommendation with some confidence. For years we have been working with alcoholics committed to institutions. Since this book was first published, A.A. has released thousands of alcoholics from asylums and hospitals of every kind. The majority have never returned. The power of fellowship and personal growth goes deep!

You may have the reverse situation on your hands. Perhaps you have a spouse who is at large, but who should be committed. Some people cannot or will not get over alcoholism. When they become too dangerous, we think the kind thing is to lock them up, but of course a good doctor should always be consulted. The wives, husbands and children of such alcoholics suffer horribly, but not more than the alcoholic themselves.

But sometimes you must start life anew. We know many people who have done it. If such people adopt a spiritual way of life their road will be smoother.

If your spouse is a drinker, you probably worry over what other people are thinking and you hate to meet your friends. You draw more and more into yourself and you think everyone is talking about conditions at your home. You avoid the subject of drinking, even with your own parents. You do not know what to tell the children. When your spouse is bad, you become a trembling recluse, wishing the telephone had never been invented.

We find that most of this embarrassment is unnecessary. While you need not discuss your partner at length, you can quietly let your friends know the nature of their illness. But you must be on guard not to embarrass or harm your spouse.

When you have carefully explained to such people that they are a sick person, you will have created a new atmosphere. Barriers which have sprung up between you and your friends will disappear with the growth of sympathetic understanding. You will no longer be self-conscious or feel that you must apologize as though your spouse were a weak character. They may be anything but that. Your new courage, good nature and lack of self-consciousness will do wonders for you socially.

The same principle applies in dealing with the children. Unless they actually need protection from their alcoholic parent, it is best not to take sides in any argument they have with them while drinking. Use your energies to promote a better understanding all around. Then that terrible tension which grips the home of every problem drinker will be lessened.

Frequently, you have felt obliged to tell your spouse's employer and their friends that they were sick, when as a matter of fact they were tight. Avoid answering these inquiries as much as you can. Whenever possible, let your spouse explain. Your desire to protect them should not cause you to lie to people when they have a right to know where they are and what they are doing. Discuss this with them when they are sober and in good spirits. Ask them what you should do if they place you in such a position again. But be careful not to be resentful about the last time they did so.

There is another paralyzing fear. You may be afraid your spouse will lose their position; you are thinking of the disgrace and hard times which will befall you and the children. This experience may come to you. Or you may already have had it several times. Should it happen again, regard it in a different light. Maybe it will prove a good thing! It may convince your spouse they want to stop drinking forever. And now you know that they can stop if they will! Time after time, this apparent calamity has been a boon to us, for it opened up a path which led to the discovery of spiritual principles.

We have elsewhere remarked how much better life is when lived on a spiritual plane. If this kind of life can solve the age-old riddle of alcoholism, it can solve your problems too. We spouses found that, like everybody else, we were afflicted with pride, self-pity, vanity and all the things which go to make up the self-centered person; and we were not above selfishness or dishonesty. As our wives and husbands began to apply spiritual principles in their lives, we began to see the desirability of doing so too.

At first, some of us did not believe we needed this help. We thought, on the whole, we were pretty good people, capable of being nicer if our partners stopped drinking. But it was a silly idea that we were too good to need spiritual principles. Now we try to put these principles to work in every department of our lives. When we do that, we find it solves our problems too; the ensuing lack of fear, worry and hurt feelings is a wonderful thing. We urge you to try our program, for nothing will be so helpful to your spouse as the radically changed attitude toward them which this will show you how to have. Go along with your spouse if you possibly can.

If you and your partner find a solution for the pressing problem of drink you are, of course, going to be very happy. But all problems will not be solved at once. Seed has started to sprout in a new soil, but growth has only begun. In spite of your new-found happiness, there will be ups and downs. Many of the old problems will still be with you. This is as it should be.

The sincerity of both you and your spouse will be put to the test. These workouts should be regarded as part of your education, for thus you will be learning to live. You will make mistakes, but if you are in earnest they will not drag you down. Instead, you will capitalize them. A better way of life will emerge when they are overcome.

Some of the snags you will encounter are irritation, hurt feelings and resentments. Your spouse will sometimes be unreasonable and you will want to criticize. Starting from a speck on the domestic horizon, great thunderclouds of dispute may gather. These family dissensions are very dangerous, especially to your spouse. Often you must carry the burden of avoiding them or keeping them under control. Never forget that resentment is a deadly hazard to an alcoholic. We do not mean that you have to agree with your spouse whenever there is an honest difference of opinion. Just be careful not to disagree in a resentful or critical spirit.

You and your partner will find that you can dispose of serious problems easier than you can the trivial ones. Next time you have a heated discussion, no matter what the subject, it should be the privilege of either to smile and say, "This is getting serious. I'm sorry I got disturbed. Let's talk about it later." If your spouse is trying to live on a spiritual basis, they will also be doing everything in their power to avoid disagreement or contention.

Your spouse knows they owe you more than sobriety. They want to make good. Yet you must not expect too much. Their way of thinking and doing are the habits of years. Patience, tolerance, understanding and love are the watchwords. Show them these things in yourself and they will be reflected back to you. Live and let live is the rule. If you both show a willingness to remedy your own defects, there will be little need to criticize each other.

We carry with us a picture of the ideal person, the sort we would like our spouses to be. It is the most natural thing in the world, once their liquor problem is solved, to feel that they will now measure up to that cherished vision. The chances are they will not for, like yourself, they are just beginning their development. Be patient.

Another feeling we are very likely to entertain is one of resentment that love and loyalty could not cure our spouses of alcoholism. We do not like the thought that the contents of a book or the work of another alcoholic has accomplished in a few weeks that for which we struggled for years. At such moments we forget that alcoholism is an illness over which we could not possibly have had any power. Your spouse will be the first to say it was your devotion and care which brought them to the point where they could have a spiritual experience. Without you they would have gone to pieces long ago. When resentful thoughts come, try to pause and be grateful. After all, your family is reunited, alcohol is no longer a problem and you and your partner are working together toward an undreamed of future.

Still another difficulty is that you may become jealous of the attention they bestow on other people, especially alcoholics.

You have been starving for their companionship, yet they spend long hours helping other people and their families. You feel they should now be yours. The fact is that they should work with other people to maintain their own sobriety. Sometimes they will be so interested that they become really neglectful. Your house is filled with strangers. You may not like some of them. They get stirred up about their troubles, but not at all about yours. It will do little good if you point that out and urge more attention for yourself. We find it a real mistake to dampen their enthusiasm for alcoholic work. You should join in their efforts as much as you possibly can. We suggest that you direct some of your thought to the partners of their new alcoholic friends. They need the counsel and love of a person who has gone through what you have.

It is probably true that you and your spouse have been living too much alone, for drinking many times isolates the spouse of an alcoholic. Therefore, you probably need fresh interests and a great cause to live for as much as your spouse. If you cooperate, rather than complain, you will find that their excess enthusiasm will tone down. Both of you will awaken to a new sense of responsibility for others. You, as well as your spouse, ought to think of what you can put into life instead of how much you can take out. Inevitably your lives will be fuller for doing so. You will lose the old life to find one much better.

Perhaps your spouse will make a fair start on the new basis, but just as things are going beautifully they dismay you by coming home drunk. If you are satisfied they really want to get over drinking, you need not be alarmed. Though it is infinitely better that they have no relapse at all, as has been true with many of our members, it is by no means a bad thing in some cases. Your spouse will see at once that they must redouble their spiritual activities if they expect to survive. You need not remind them of their spiritual deficiency—they will know of it. Cheer them up and ask them how you can be still more helpful.

The slightest sign of fear or intolerance may lessen your spouse's chance of recovery. In a weak moment they may take your dislike of their high-stepping friends as one of those insanely trivial excuses to drink.

We never, never try to arrange a person's life so as to shield them from temptation. The slightest disposition on your part to guide their appointments or affairs so they will not be tempted will be noticed. Make them feel absolutely free to come and go as they like. This is important. If they get drunk, don't blame yourself. Your spouse's liquor problem has either been removed or it has not. If not, it had better be found out right away. Then you and your spouse can get right down to fundamentals. If a repetition is to be prevented, continue to hope for the alcoholic's recovery and work towards that end.

We realize that we have been giving you much direction and advice. We may have seemed to lecture. If that is so we are sorry, for we ourselves don't always care for people who lecture us. But what we have related is based upon experience, some of it painful. We had to learn these things the hard way. That is why we are anxious that you understand, and that you avoid these unnecessary difficulties.*

So to you out there who may soon be with us—we say "Good luck and best wishes to you and your spouse!"

The fellowship of Al-Anon Family Groups was formed about 13 years after this chapter was written. Though it is entirely separate from Alcoholics Anonymous, it uses the general principles of the A.A. program as a guide for husbands, wives, relatives, friends, and others close to alcoholics. The foregoing pages (though addressed only to spouses) indicate the problems such people may face. Alateen, for teen-aged children of alcoholics, is a part of Al-Anon.

If there is no Al-Anon listing in your local telephone book, you may obtain further information on Al-Anon/Alateen Family Groups by writing to its World Service Office, 1600 Corporate Landing Parkway, Virginia Beach, VA 23454-5617.

Chapter 9

To The Family

OUR SPOUSES have suggested certain attitudes a husband or wife may take with the alcoholic who is recovering. Perhaps they created the impression that the alcoholic is to be wrapped in cotton wool and placed on a pedestal. Successful readjustment means the opposite. All members of the family should meet upon the common ground of tolerance, understanding and love. This involves a process of deflation. The alcoholic, the spouse, the children, the "in-laws," each one is likely to have fixed ideas about the family's attitude towards himself or herself. Each is interested in having his or her wishes respected. We find the more one member of the family demands that the others concede to the alcoholic, the more resentful they become. This makes for discord and unhappiness.

Commentary: I won't even mention that the original text started this chapter with "Our women folk ..." Oh ... wait ... okay ... I did. Now that I have mentioned it, I will say this is incredibly archaic language. This kind of terminology has gone past amusing and has now arrived at being utterly repugnant. If I were a woman of a certain attitude, I would be throwing the Big Book into the trash can right now. There is no sane way the Big Book can be so precious that this kind of ridiculous language should remain. With every passing day, the original text is losing relevance and, with it, many who would benefit from a 21st century version.

And why? Is it not because each wants to play the lead? Is not each trying to arrange the family show to their liking? Are they not unconsciously trying to see what they can take from the family life rather than give?

Cessation of drinking is but the first step away from a highly strained, abnormal condition. A doctor said to us, "Years of living with an alcoholic is almost sure to make any spouse or child neurotic. The entire family is, to some extent, ill." Let families realize, as they start their journey, that all will not be fair weather. Each in their turn may be footsore and may straggle. There will be alluring shortcuts and by-paths down which they may wander and lose their way.

Suppose we tell you some of the obstacles a family will meet; suppose we suggest how they may be avoided—even converted to good use for others. The family of an alcoholic longs for the return of happiness and security. They remember when the alcoholic was romantic, thoughtful and successful. Today's life is measured against that of other years and, when it falls short, the family may be unhappy.

Family confidence in the alcoholic is rising high. The good old days will soon be back, they think. Sometimes they demand that they bring them back instantly! They believe they are owed this recompense on a long overdue account. But the alcoholic has spent years in pulling down the structures of business, romance, friendship, health—these things are now ruined or damaged. It will take time to clear away the wreck. Though old buildings will eventually be replaced by finer ones, the new structures will take years to complete.

The alcoholic knows they are to blame; it may take them many seasons of hard work to be restored financially, but they shouldn't be reproached. Perhaps they will never have much money again. But the wise family will admire them for what they are trying to be, rather than for what they are trying to get.

Now and then the family will be plagued by spectres from the past, for the drinking career of almost every alcoholic has been marked by escapades, funny, humiliating, shameful or tragic. The first impulse will be to bury these skeletons in a dark closet and padlock the door. The family may be possessed by the idea that future happiness can be based only upon forgetfulness of the past. We think that such a view is self-centered and in direct conflict with the new way of living.

Henry Ford once made a wise remark to the effect that experience is the thing of supreme value in life. That is true only if one is willing to turn the past to good account. We grow by our willingness to face and rectify errors and convert them into assets. The alcoholic's past thus becomes the principal asset of the family and frequently it is almost the only one!

This painful past may be of infinite value to other families still struggling with their problem. We think each family which has been relieved owes something to those who have not, and when the occasion requires, each member of it should be only too willing to bring former mistakes, no matter how grievous, out of their hiding places. Showing others who suffer how we were given help is the very thing which makes life seem so worth while to us now. Cling to the thought that the dark past is one of the greatest possessions you have—the key to life and happiness for others. With it you can avert death and misery for them.

It is possible to dig up past misdeeds so they become a blight, a veritable plague. For example, we know of situations in which the alcoholic or their spouse have had love affairs. In the first flush of spiritual experience they forgave each other and drew closer together. Reconciliation was at hand. Then, under one provocation or another, the aggrieved one would unearth the old affair and angrily cast its ashes about. A few of us have had these growing pains and they hurt a great deal. Husbands and wives have sometimes been obliged to separate for a time until new perspective, new victory over hurt pride could be rewon. In most cases, the alcoholic survived this ordeal without relapse, but not always. So we think that unless some good and useful purpose is to be served, past occurrences should not be discussed.

We families of Alcoholics Anonymous keep few skeletons in the closet. Everyone knows about the others' alcoholic troubles. This is a condition which, in ordinary life, would produce untold grief; there might be scandalous gossip, laughter at the expense of other people, and a tendency to take advantage of intimate information. Among us, these are rare occurrences. We do talk about each other a great deal, but we almost invariably temper such talk by a spirit of love and tolerance.

Another principle we observe carefully is that we do not relate intimate experiences of another person unless we are sure they would approve. We find it better, when possible, to stick to our own stories. A person may criticize or laugh at themselves and it will affect others favorably, but criticism or ridicule coming from another often produces the contrary effect. Members of a family should watch such matters carefully, for one careless, inconsiderate remark has been known to raise problems. We alcoholics are sensitive people. It takes some of us a long time to outgrow that serious handicap.

Many alcoholics are enthusiasts. They run to extremes. At the beginning of recovery a person will take, as a rule, one of two directions. They may either plunge into a frantic attempt to get on their feet in business, or they may be so enthralled by this new life that they talk or think of little else. In either case certain family problems will arise. With these we have had experience galore.

We think it dangerous if they rush headlong at their economic problem. The family will be affected also, pleasantly at first, as they feel their money troubles are about to be solved, then not so pleasantly as they find themselves neglected. The alcoholic may be tired at night and preoccupied by day. They may take small interest in the children and may show irritation when reproved for their delinquencies. If not irritable, they may seem dull and boring, not gay and affectionate as the family would like them to be. The spouse may complain of inattention. They are all disappointed, and often let the alcoholic feel it. Beginning with such complaints, a barrier arises. The alcoholic is straining every nerve to make up for lost time. They are striving to recover fortune and reputation and feel they are doing very well.

Sometimes the spouse and children don't think so. Having been neglected and misused in the past, they think the alcoholic owes them more than they are getting. They want the alcoholic to make a fuss over them. They expect the alcoholic to give them the nice times they used to have before they drank so much, and to show their contrition for what they suffered. But the alcoholic doesn't give freely of themselves. Resentment grows. The alcoholic becomes still less communicative. Sometimes they explode over a trifle. The family is mystified. They criticize, pointing out how the alcoholic is falling down on their spiritual program.

This sort of thing can be avoided. Both the alcoholic and the family are mistaken, though each side may have some justification. It is of little use to argue and only makes the impasse worse. The family must realize that the alcoholic, though marvelously improved, is still convalescing. They should be thankful the alcoholic is sober and able to be of this world once more. Let them praise the alcoholic's progress. Let them remember that their drinking wrought all kinds of damage that may take long to repair. If they sense these things, they will not take so seriously the alcoholic's periods of crankiness, depression, or apathy, which will disappear when there is tolerance, love, and spiritual understanding.

The alcoholic ought to remember that they are mainly to blame for what befell their home. They can scarcely square the account in their lifetime. But they must see the danger of over-concentration on financial success. Although financial recovery is on the way for many of us, we found we could not place money first. For us, material well being always followed spiritual progress; it never preceded.

Since the home has suffered more than anything else, it is well that an alcoholic exert themselves there. They are not likely to get far in any direction if they fail to show unselfishness and love under their own roof. We know there are difficult spouses and families, but the person who is getting over alcoholism must remember they did much to make them so.

As each member of a resentful family begins to see their shortcomings and admits them to the others, they lay a basis for helpful discussion. These family talks will be constructive if they can be carried on without heated argument, self-pity, self-justification or resentful criticism. Little by little, the family will see they ask too much, and the alcoholic will see they give too little. Giving, rather than getting, will become the guiding principle.

Assume on the other hand that the alcoholic has, at the outset, a stirring spiritual experience. Overnight, as it were, they are a different person. Maybe they become a religious enthusiast. They are unable to focus on anything else. As soon as their sobriety begins to be taken as a matter of course, the family may look at their strange new dad or mother with apprehension, then with irritation. There is talk about spiritual matters morning, noon and night. They may demand that the family find god in a hurry, or exhibit amazing indifference to them and say they are above worldly considerations. They may tell their spouse, who is not religious, that they don't know what it's all about, and that they had better get the alcoholic's brand of spirituality while there is yet time.

When the alcoholic takes this tack, the family may react unfavorably. They may be jealous of a god who has stolen the alcoholic's affections. While grateful that the alcoholic drinks no more, they may not like the idea that this god has accomplished the "miracle" where they failed. They often forget that some alcoholics feel they are beyond human aid. They may not see why their love and devotion did not straighten the alcoholic out. The alcoholic is not so spiritual after all, they say. If they mean to right their past wrongs, why all this concern for everyone in the world but their family? What about this talk that god will take care of them? They suspect the alcoholic is a bit balmy!

The alcoholic is not so unbalanced as they might think. Many of us have experienced the same elation. We have indulged in spiritual intoxication. Like a gaunt prospector, belt drawn in over the last ounce of food, our pick struck gold. Joy at our release from a lifetime of frustration knew no bounds. They feel they have struck something better than gold. For a time they may try to hug the new treasure to themselves. They may not see at once that they have barely scratched a limitless lode which will pay dividends only if they mine it for the rest of their life and insists on giving away the entire product.

If the family cooperates, the alcoholic will soon see that they are suffering from a distortion of values. They will perceive that their spiritual growth is lopsided, that for an average person like themselves, a spiritual life which does not include the family obligations may not be so perfect after all. If the family will appreciate that the alcoholic's current behavior is but a phase of their development, all will be well. In the midst of an understanding and sympathetic family, these vagaries of the alcoholic's spiritual infancy will quickly disappear.

The opposite may happen should the family condemn and criticize. The alcoholic may feel that for years their drinking has placed them on the wrong side of every argument, but that now they have become a superior person with god on their side. If the family persists in criticism, this fallacy may take a still greater hold on the alcoholic. Instead of treating the family as they should, they may retreat further into themselves and feel they have spiritual justification for so doing.

Though the family does not fully agree with the alcoholic's spiritual activities, they should let them have their head. Even if they display a certain amount of neglect and irresponsibility towards the family, it is well to let them go as far as they like in helping other alcoholics. During those first days of convalescence, this will do more to insure their sobriety than anything else. Though some of their manifestations are alarming and disagreeable, we think they will be on a firmer foundation than the person who is placing business or professional success ahead of spiritual development. He will be less likely to drink again, and anything is preferable to that.

Those of us who have spent much time in the world of spiritual make-believe have eventually seen the childishness of it. This dream world has been replaced by a great sense of purpose, accompanied by a growing consciousness of a power greater than ourselves in our lives. We have come to believe that keeping our heads in the clouds doesn't work. Instead our feet ought to be firmly planted on earth. That is where our fellow travelers are, and that is where our work must be done. These are the realities for us. We have found nothing incompatible between a powerful spiritual experience and a life of sane and happy usefulness.

One more suggestion: Whether the family has spiritual convictions or not, they may do well to examine the principles by which the alcoholic member is trying to live. They can hardly fail to approve these simple principles, though the alcoholic still fails somewhat in practicing them. Nothing will help the person who is off on a spiritual tangent so much as the spouse who adopts a sane spiritual program, making a better practical use of it.

There will be other profound changes in the household. Liquor incapacitated the alcoholic for so many years that the spouse became head of the house. They met these responsibilities gallantly. By force of circumstances, they were often obliged to treat the alcoholic as a sick or wayward child. Even when they wanted to assert themselves they could not, for their drinking placed them constantly in the wrong. The spouse of the alcoholic made all the plans and gave the directions. When sober, the alcoholic usually obeyed. Thus the spouse, through no fault of their own, became accustomed to being in charge. The alcoholic, coming suddenly to life again, often begins to assert themselves. This means trouble, unless the family watches for these tendencies in each other and comes to a friendly agreement about them.

Drinking isolates most homes from the outside world. The alcoholic may have laid aside for years all normal activities—clubs, civic duties, sports. When they renew interest in such things, a feeling of jealousy may arise. The family may feel they hold a mortgage on the alcoholic, so big that no equity should be left for outsiders. Instead of developing new channels of activity for themselves, the family demands that the alcoholic stay home and make up the deficiency.

At the very beginning, the couple ought to frankly face the fact that each will have to yield here and there if the family is going to play an effective part in the new life. The alcoholic will necessarily spend much time with other alcoholics, but this activity should be balanced. New acquaintances who know nothing of alcoholism might be made and thoughtful consideration given their needs. The problems of the community might engage attention. If the family has no religious connections, there is no need to make contact with or take membership in a religious body. If you are religious, by all means, do so.

Alcoholics who have derided religious people will find there is no need for such judgements. Being possessed of a spiritual experience, the alcoholic will find they have much in common with these people, though they may differ with them on many matters. If they do not argue about religion, they will make new friends and are sure to find new avenues of usefulness and pleasure. We intend the foregoing as a helpful suggestion only. So far as we are concerned, there is nothing obligatory about it. As religious and non-religious people, we cannot make up others' minds for them. Each individual should consult their own conscience.

We have been speaking to you of serious, sometimes tragic things. We have been dealing with alcohol in its worst aspect. But we aren't a glum lot. If newcomers could see no joy or fun in our existence, they wouldn't want it. We absolutely insist on enjoying life. We try not to indulge in cynicism over the state of the nations, nor do we carry the world's troubles on our shoulders. When we see a person sinking into the mire that is alcoholism, we give them first aid and place what we have at their disposal. For their sake, we do recount and almost relive the horrors of our past. But those of us who have tried to shoulder the entire burden and trouble of others find we are soon overcome by them.

So we think cheerfulness and laughter make for usefulness. Outsiders are sometimes shocked when we burst into merriment over a seemingly tragic experience out of the past. But why shouldn't we laugh? We have recovered, and have been given the power to help others.

Everybody knows that those in bad health, and those who seldom play, do not laugh much. So let each family play together or separately, as much as their circumstances warrant. We want to be happy, joyous, and free. We cannot subscribe to the belief that this life is a vale of tears, though it once was just that for many of us. But it is clear that we made our own misery. Avoid then, the deliberate manufacture of misery, but if trouble comes, cheerfully capitalize it as an opportunity for personal growth.

Now about health: A body badly burned by alcohol does not often recover overnight nor do twisted thinking and depression vanish in a twinkling. We are convinced that a spiritual mode of living is a most powerful health restorative. We, who have recovered from serious drinking, may be good examples of mental health. But we have seen remarkable transformations in our bodies, too. Hardly one of our crowd now shows any mark of dissipation.

But this does not mean that we disregard human health measures. This world is abundantly supplied with fine doctors, psychologists, and practitioners of various kinds. Do not hesitate to take your health problems to such persons. Most of them give freely of themselves, that their fellows may enjoy sound minds and bodies. Try to remember that we should never belittle a good doctor or psychiatrist. Their services are often indispensable in treating a newcomer and in following their case afterward.

One of the many doctors who had the opportunity of reading this book in manuscript form told us that the use of sweets was often helpful, of course depending upon a doctor's advice. They thought all alcoholics should constantly have chocolate available for its quick energy value at times of fatigue. They added that occasionally in the night a vague craving arose which would be satisfied by candy. Many of us have noticed a tendency to eat sweets and have found this practice beneficial.

A word about sex relations. Alcohol is so sexually stimulating to some that they have over-indulged. Couples are occasionally dismayed to find that when drinking is stopped the alcoholic becomes disinterested. The reason may be an emotional upset. Some of us had this experience, only to enjoy, in a few months, a finer intimacy than ever. There should be no hesitancy in consulting a doctor or psychologist if this persists. We do not know of many cases where this difficulty lasted long.

The alcoholic may find it hard to re-establish friendly relations with their children. Their young minds were impressionable while they were drinking. Without saying so, they may cordially hate the alcoholic parent for what they have done to them and to their mother or father. The children are sometimes dominated by a pathetic hardness and cynicism. They cannot seem to forgive and forget. This may hang on for months, long after their other parent has accepted the alcoholic's new way of living and thinking.

In time they will see that the alcoholic is a new person and in their own way they will let them know it. When this happens, they can be invited to join in morning meditation and then they can take part in the daily discussion without rancor or bias. From that point on, progress will be rapid. Marvelous results often follow such a reunion.

Whether the family goes on a spiritual basis or not, the alcoholic member has to if they would recover. The others must be convinced of the alcoholic's new status beyond the shadow of a doubt. Seeing is believing to most families who have lived with a drinker.

Here is a case in point: One of our friends is a heavy smoker and coffee drinker. There was no doubt she over-indulged. Seeing this, and meaning to be helpful, her husband commenced to admonish her about it. She admitted she was overdoing these things, but frankly said that she was not ready to stop. Her husband is one of those persons who really feels there is something quite wrong about these commodities, so he nagged, and his intolerance finally threw her into a fit of anger. She got drunk.

Of course our friend was wrong—dead wrong. She had to painfully admit that and mend her spiritual fences. Though she is now a most effective member of Alcoholics Anonymous, she still smokes and drinks coffee, but neither her husband nor anyone else stands in judgment. He sees he was wrong to make a burning issue out of such a matter when her more serious ailments were being rapidly cured.

We have three little mottoes which are apropos. Here they are:

First Things First
Live and Let Live
Easy Does It.

Chapter 10

To The Employer

AMONG MANY employers nowadays, we think of one member who has spent much of his life in the world of big business. He has hired and fired hundreds of people. He knows the alcoholic as the employer sees them. His present views ought to prove exceptionally useful to business people everywhere.

But let him tell you:

I was at one time assistant manager of a corporation department employing sixty-six hundred people. One day my secretary came in saying that Mr. B—insisted on speaking with me. I told the secretary to say that I was not interested. I had warned him several times that he had but one more chance. Not long afterward he had called me from Hartford on two successive days, so drunk he could hardly speak. I told him he was through—finally and forever.

My secretary returned to say that it was not Mr. B—on the phone; it was Mr. B—'s brother, and he wished to give me a message. I still expected a plea for clemency, but these words came through the receiver: "I just wanted to tell you Paul jumped from a hotel window in Hartford last Saturday. He left us a note saying you were the best boss he ever had, and that you were not to blame in any way."

Another time, as I opened a letter which lay on my desk, a newspaper clipping fell out. It was the obituary of one of the best salespeople I ever had. After two weeks of drinking, they had placed their toe on the trigger of a loaded shotgun—the barrel was in their mouth. I had discharged them for drinking six weeks before.

Still another experience: A man's voice came faintly over long distance from Virginia. He wanted to know if his wife's company insurance was still in force. Four days before she had hanged herself. I had been obliged to discharge her for drinking, though she was brilliant, alert, and one of the best organizers I have ever known.

Here were three exceptional people lost to this world because I did not understand alcoholism as I do now. What irony—I became an alcoholic myself! And but for the intervention of an understanding person, I might have followed in their footsteps. My downfall cost the business community unknown thousands of dollars, for it takes real money to train a person for an executive position. This kind of waste goes on unabated. We think the business fabric is shot through with a situation which might be helped by better understanding all around.

Nearly every modern employer feels a responsibility for the well-being of their help, and they try to meet these responsibilities. That they have not always done so for the alcoholic is easily understood. To them the alcoholic has often seemed a fool of the first magnitude. Because of the employee's special ability, or of their own strong personal attachment to them, the employer has sometimes kept such a person at work long beyond a reasonable period. Some employers have tried every known remedy. In only a few instances has there been a lack of patience and tolerance. And we, who have imposed on the best of employers, can scarcely blame them if they have been short with us.

Here, for instance, is a typical example: An officer of one of the largest banking institutions in America knows I no longer drink. One day she told me about an executive of the same bank who, from her description, was undoubtedly alcoholic. This seemed to me like an opportunity to be helpful, so I spent two hours talking about alcoholism, the malady, and described the symptoms and results as well as I could. Her comment was, "Very interesting. But I'm sure this person is done drinking. They have just returned from a three-months leave of absence, have taken a cure, looks fine, and to clinch the matter, the board of directors told them this was their last chance."

The only answer I could make was that if the person followed the usual pattern, they would go on a bigger bust than ever. I felt this was inevitable and wondered if the bank was doing the person an injustice. Why not bring them into contact with some of our alcoholic crowd? They might have a chance. I pointed out that I had had nothing to drink whatever for three years, and this in the face of difficulties that would have made nine out of ten people drink their heads off. Why not at least afford them an opportunity to hear my story? "Oh no," said my friend, "this one is either through with liquor, or they are minus a job. If they have your will power and guts, they will make the grade."

I wanted to throw up my hands in discouragement, for I saw that I had failed to help my banker friend understand. She simply could not believe that her employee suffered from a serious illness. There was nothing to do but wait.

Presently the person did slip and was fired. Following their discharge, we contacted them. Without much ado, they accepted the principles and procedure that had helped us. They are undoubtedly on the road to recovery. To me, this incident illustrates lack of understanding as to what really ails the alcoholic, and lack of knowledge as to what part employers might profitably take in salvaging their sick employees.

If you desire to help it might be well to disregard your own drinking, or lack of it. Whether you are a hard drinker, a moderate drinker or a teetotaler, you may have some pretty strong opinions, perhaps prejudices. Those who drink moderately may be more annoyed with an alcoholic than a total abstainer would be. Drinking occasionally, and understanding your own reactions, it is possible for you to become quite sure of many things which, so far as the alcoholic is concerned, are not always so. As a moderate drinker, you can take your liquor or leave it alone. Whenever you want to, you control your drinking. Of an evening, you can go on a mild bender, get up in the morning, shake your head and go to business. To you, liquor is no real problem. You cannot see why it should be to anyone else, save the spineless and stupid.

When dealing with an alcoholic, there may be a natural

annoyance that a person could be so weak, stupid and irresponsible. Even when you understand the malady better, you may feel this feeling rising.

A look at the alcoholic in your organization is many times illuminating. Are they not usually brilliant, fast thinking, imaginative and likable? When sober, do they not work hard and have a knack of getting things done? If they had these qualities and did not drink would they be worth retaining? Should they have the same consideration as other ailing employees? Are they worth salvaging? If your decision is yes, whether the reason be humanitarian or business or both, then the following suggestions may be helpful.

Can you discard the feeling that you are dealing only with habit, with stubbornness, or a weak will? If this presents difficulty, re-reading chapters two and three, where the alcoholic sickness is discussed at length might be worthwhile. You, as a businessperson, want to know the necessities before considering the result. If you concede that your employee is ill, can they be forgiven for what they have done in the past? Can their past absurdities be forgotten? Can it be appreciated that they have been a victim of crooked thinking, directly caused by the action of alcohol on their brain?

I well remember the shock I received when a prominent doctor in Chicago told me of cases where pressure of the spinal fluid actually ruptured the brain. No wonder an alcoholic is strangely irrational. Who wouldn't be, with such a fevered brain? Normal drinkers are not so affected, nor can they understand the aberrations of the alcoholic.

Your employee has probably been trying to conceal a number of scrapes, perhaps pretty messy ones. They may be disgusting. You may be at a loss to understand how such a seemingly above-board person could be so involved. But these scrapes can generally be charged, no matter how bad, to the abnormal action of alcohol on their mind. When drinking, or getting over a bout, an alcoholic, sometimes the model of honesty when normal, will do incredible things. Afterward, their revulsion will be terrible. Nearly always, these antics indicate nothing more than temporary conditions.

This is not to say that all alcoholics are honest and upright when not drinking. Of course that isn't so, and such people often may impose on you. Seeing your attempt to understand and help, some will try to take advantage of your kindness. If you are sure your employee does not want to stop, they may as well be discharged, the sooner the better. You are not doing them a favor by keeping them on. Firing such an individual may prove to be the best thing for them. It may be just the jolt they need. I know, in my own particular case, that nothing my company could have done would have stopped me for, so long as I was able to hold my position, I could not possibly realize how serious my situation was. Had they fired me first, and had they then taken steps to see that I was presented with the solution contained in this book, I might have returned to them six months later, a well man.

But there are many people who want to stop, and with them you can go far. Your understanding treatment of their cases will pay dividends.

Perhaps you have such a person in mind. They want to quit drinking and you want to help them, even if it be only a matter of good business. You now know more about alcoholism. You can see that they are mentally and physically sick. You are willing to overlook their past performances. Suppose an approach is made something like this:

State that you know about their drinking, and that it must stop. You might say you appreciate their abilities, would like to keep them, but cannot if they continue to drink. A firm attitude at this point has helped many of us.

Next they can be assured that you do not intend to lecture, moralize, or condemn; that if this was done formerly, it was because of misunderstanding. If possible express a lack of hard feeling toward them. At this point, it might be well to explain alcoholism, the illness. Say that you believe they are a gravely ill person, with this qualification—being perhaps fatally ill, do they want to get well? You ask, because many alcoholics, being warped and drugged, do not want to quit. But do they? Will they take every necessary step, submit to anything to get well, to stop drinking forever?

If they say yes, do they really mean it, or down inside do they think they are fooling you, and that after rest and treatment they will be able to get away with a few drinks now and then? We believe a person should be thoroughly probed on these points. Be satisfied they are not deceiving themselves or you.

Whether you mention this book is a matter for your discretion. If they temporize and still think they can ever drink again, even beer, they might as well be discharged after the next bender which, if an alcoholic, they are almost certain to have. They should understand that emphatically. Either you are dealing with a person who can and will get well or you are not. If not, why waste time with them? This may seem severe, but it is usually the best course.

After satisfying yourself that your employee wants to recover and that they will go to any extreme to do so, you may suggest a definite course of action. For most alcoholics who are drinking, or who are just getting over a spree, a certain amount of physical treatment is desirable, even imperative. The matter of physical treatment should, of course, be referred to your own doctor. Whatever the method, its object is to thoroughly clear mind and body of the effects of alcohol. In competent hands, this seldom takes long nor is it very expensive. Your employee will fare better if placed in such physical condition that they can think straight and no longer crave liquor. If you propose such a procedure to them, it may be necessary to advance the cost of treatment, but we believe it should be made plain that any expense will later be deducted from their pay. It is better for them to feel fully responsible.

If your employee accepts your offer, it should be pointed out that physical treatment is but a small part of the picture. Though you are providing them with the best possible medical attention, they should understand that they must undergo a change of heart. To get over drinking will require a transformation of thought and attitude. We all had to place recovery above everything, for without recovery we would have lost both home and business.

Can you have every confidence in their ability to recover? While on the subject of confidence, can you adopt the attitude that so far as you are concerned this will be a strictly personal matter, that their alcoholic derelictions, the treatment about to be undertaken, will never be discussed without their consent? It might be well to have a long chat with them on their return.

To return to the subject matter of this book: It contains full suggestions by which the employee may solve their problem. To you, some of the ideas which it contains are novel. Perhaps you are not quite in sympathy with the approach we suggest. By no means do we offer it as the last word on this subject, but so far as we are concerned, it has worked with us. After all, are you not looking for results rather than methods? Whether your employee likes it or not, they will learn the grim truth about alcoholism. That won't hurt them a bit, even though they do not go for this remedy.

We suggest you draw the book to the attention of the doctor who is to attend your patient during treatment. If the book is read the moment the patient is able, while acutely depressed, realization of their condition may come to them.

We hope the doctor will tell the patient the truth about their condition, whatever that happens to be. When the person is presented with this volume it is best that no one tell them they must abide by its suggestions. The person must decide for themselves.

You are betting, of course, that your changed attitude plus the contents of this book will turn the trick. In some cases it will, and in others it may not. But we think that if you persevere, the percentage of successes will gratify you. As our work spreads and our numbers increase, we hope your employees may be put in personal contact with some of us. Meanwhile, we are sure a great deal can be accomplished by the use of the book alone.

On your employee's return, talk with them. Ask them if they think they have the answer. If they feel free to discuss their problems with you, if they know you understand and will not be upset by anything they wish to say, they will probably be off to a fast start.

In this connection, can you remain undisturbed if the person proceeds to tell you shocking things? They may, for example, reveal that they have padded their expense account or that they have planned to take your best customers away from you. In fact, they may say almost anything if they have accepted our solution which, as you know, demands rigorous honesty. Can you charge this off as you would a bad account and start fresh with them? If they owe you money you may wish to make terms.

If they speak of their home situation, you can undoubtedly make helpful suggestions. Can they talk frankly with you so long as they do not bear business tales or criticize their associates? With this kind of employee such an attitude will command undying loyalty.

The greatest enemies of us alcoholics are resentment, jealousy, envy, frustration, and fear. Wherever people are gathered together in business there will be rivalries and, arising out of these, a certain amount of office politics. Sometimes we alcoholics have an idea that people are trying to pull us down. Often this is not so at all. But sometimes our drinking will be used politically.

One instance comes to mind in which a malicious individual was always making friendly little jokes about an alcoholic's drinking exploits. In this way they were slyly carrying tales. In another case, an alcoholic was sent to a hospital for treatment. Only a few knew of it at first but, within a short time, it was bill boarded throughout the entire company. Naturally this sort of thing decreased the person's chance of recovery. The employer can many times protect the victim from this kind of talk. The employer cannot play favorites, but they can always defend a person from needless provocation and unfair criticism.

As a class, alcoholics are energetic people. They work hard and they play hard. Your employee should be on their mettle to make good. Being somewhat weakened, and faced with physical and mental readjustment to a life which knows no alcohol, they may overdo. You may have to curb their desire to work sixteen hours a day. You may need to encourage them to play once in a while. They may wish to do a lot for other alcoholics and something of the sort may come up during business hours. A reasonable amount of latitude will be helpful. This work is necessary to maintain their sobriety.

After your employee has gone along without drinking for a few months, you may be able to make use of their services with other employees who are giving you the alcoholic run-around —provided, of course, they are willing to have a third party in the picture. An alcoholic who has recovered, but holds a relatively unimportant job, can talk to a person with a better position. Being on a radically different basis of life, they will never take advantage of the situation.

Your employee may be trusted. Long experience with alcoholic excuses naturally arouses suspicion. When their spouse next calls saying they are sick, you might jump to the conclusion they are drunk. If they are, and are still trying to recover, they will tell you about it even if it means the loss of their job. For they know they must be honest if they would live at all. They will appreciate knowing you are not bothering your head about them, that you are not suspicious nor are you trying to run their life so they will be shielded from temptation to drink. If they are conscientiously following the program of recovery they can go anywhere your business may call them.

In case they do stumble, even once, you will have to decide whether to let them go. If you are sure they don't mean business, there is no doubt you should discharge them. If, on the contrary, you are sure they are doing their utmost, you may wish to give them another chance. But you should feel under no obligation to keep them on, for your obligation has been well discharged already.

There is another thing you might wish to do. If your organization is a large one, your junior executives might be provided with this book. You might let them know you have no quarrel with the alcoholics of your organization. These juniors are often in a difficult position. People under them are frequently their friends. So, for one reason or another, they cover these people, hoping matters will take a turn for the better. They often jeopardize their own positions by trying to help serious drinkers who should have been fired long ago, or else given an opportunity to get well.

After reading this book, a junior executive can go to such a person and say approximately this, "Look here. Do you want to stop drinking or not? You put me on the spot every time you get drunk. It isn't fair to me or the firm. I have been learning something about alcoholism. If you are an alcoholic, you are mighty sick. You act like one. The firm wants to help you get over it, and if you are interested, there is a way out. If you take it, your past will be forgotten and the fact that you went away for treatment will not be mentioned. But if you cannot or will not stop drinking, I think you ought to resign."

Your junior executive may not agree with the contents of our book. They need not, and often should not show it to their alcoholic prospect. But at least they will understand the problem and will no longer be misled by ordinary promises. They will be able to take a position with such a person which is eminently fair and square. They will have no further reason for covering up an alcoholic employee.

It boils right down to this: No person should be fired just because they are alcoholic. If they want to stop, they should be afforded a real chance. If they cannot or do not want to stop, they should be discharged. The exceptions are few.

We think this method of approach will accomplish several things. It will permit the rehabilitation of good people. At the same time you will feel no reluctance to rid yourself of those who cannot or will not stop. Alcoholism may be causing your organization considerable damage in its waste of time, people and reputation. We hope our suggestions will help you plug up this sometimes serious leak. We think we are sensible when we urge that you stop this waste and give your worthwhile employee a chance.

The other day an approach was made to the vice president of a large industrial concern. They remarked: "I'm mighty glad you got over your drinking. But the policy of this company is not to interfere with the habits of our employees. If a person drinks so much that their job suffers, we fire them. I don't see how you can be of any help to us for, as you see, we don't have any alcoholic problem." This same company spends millions for research every year. Their cost of production is figured to a fine decimal point. They have recreational facilities. There is company insurance. There is a real interest, both humanitarian and business, in the well-being of employees. But alcoholism—well, they just don't believe they have it.

Perhaps this is a typical attitude. We, who have collectively seen a great deal of business life, at least from the alcoholic angle, had to smile at this person's sincere opinion. They might be shocked if they knew how much alcoholism is costing their organization a year. That company may harbor many actual or potential alcoholics. We believe that managers of large enterprises often have little idea how prevalent this problem is. Even if you feel your organization has no alcoholic problem, it might pay to take another look down the line. You may make some interesting discoveries.

Of course, this chapter refers to alcoholics, sick and deranged people. What our friend, the vice president, had in mind was the habitual or whoopee drinker. As to them, their policy is undoubtedly sound, but they did not distinguish between such people and the alcoholic.

Commentary: Here is another moment of humor for you. What is a "whoopee drinker"? I wonder if I was ever a whoopee drinker in my early days. Shall I point out (again) how today's alcoholic cannot relate to these old & ridiculous terms?

It is not to be expected that an alcoholic employee will receive a disproportionate amount of time and attention. They should not be made a favorite. The right kind of person, the kind who recovers, will not want this sort of thing. They will not impose. Far from it. They will work very hard and thank you to their dying day.

Today I own a little company. There are two alcoholic employees, who produce as much as five normal salespeople. But why not? They have a new attitude, and they have been saved from a living death. I have enjoyed every moment spent in getting them straightened out.*

---

*See Appendix VI—We Shall be happy to hear from you if we can be of help.Chapter 11

A Vision For All

FOR MOST normal folks, drinking means conviviality, companionship and colorful imagination.

It means release from care, boredom and worry. It is joyous intimacy with friends and a feeling that life is good. But not so with us in those last days of heavy drinking. The old pleasures were gone. They were but memories. Never could we recapture the great moments of the past. There was an insistent yearning to enjoy life as we once did and a heartbreaking obsession that some new miracle of control would enable us to do it. There was always one more attempt —and one more failure.

The less people tolerated us, the more we withdrew from society, from life itself. As we became subjects of King Alcohol, shivering denizens of his mad realm, the chilling vapor that is loneliness settled down. It thickened, ever becoming blacker. Some of us sought out sordid places, hoping to find understanding companionship and approval. Momentarily we did—then would come oblivion and the awful awakening to face the hideous Four Horsemen—Terror, Bewilderment, Frustration, Despair. Unhappy drinkers who read this page will understand!

Commentary: "As we become subjects of King Alcohol, shivering denizens of his mad realm, the chilling vapor that is loneliness settled down." The chilling vapor that is loneliness! I just have to say that is some good writing! It's so very poetic and descriptive. Can't you just feel the chill of loneliness? No, I'm not being sarcastic. I give the author an A+ for that sentence. It kind of feels like it belongs in a dark drama which is what many of our drinking lives looked like.

Now and then a serious drinker, being dry at the moment says, "I don't miss it at all. Feel better. Work better. Having a better time." As ex-problem drinkers, we smile at such a sally. We know our friend is like a child whistling in the dark to keep up their spirits. They fool themselves. Inwardly they would give anything to take half a dozen drinks and get away with them. They will presently try the old game again, for they aren't happy about their sobriety. They cannot picture life without alcohol. Some day they will be unable to imagine life either with alcohol or without it. Then they will know loneliness such as few do. They will be at the jumping-off place. They will wish for the end.

Commentary: Here is another example of ridiculous old language. What does "sally" mean? I looked it up in Webster's Dictionary. It means to rush forward or a quick retort. If I were to substitute either of these things for "sally," it still wouldn't make any sense. I believe the author means to say something like "foolishness." This sort of language invites derision and mockery. Of course, that is what I'm doing. I prefer to see it as constructive criticism. Others may see it as just throwing stones. "Maybe, if I throw more, AA can build a better foundation with them," he quickly retorted. Wouldn't it be nice if AA had a primary text that wasn't so laughable?

We have shown how we got out from under. You say, "Yes, I'm willing. But am I to be consigned to a life where I shall be stupid, boring and glum, like some righteous people I see know I must get along without liquor, but how can I? Have you a sufficient substitute?"

Yes, there is a substitute and it is vastly more than that. It is a fellowship in Alcoholics Anonymous. There you will find release from care, boredom and worry. Your imagination will be fired. Life will mean something at last. The most satisfactory years of your existence lie ahead. Thus we find the fellowship, and so will you.

"How is that to come about?" you ask. "Where am I to find these people?"

You are going to meet these new friends in your own community. Near you, alcoholics are dying helplessly like people in a sinking ship. If you live in a large place, there are hundreds. High and low, rich and poor, these are future fellows of Alcoholics Anonymous. Among them you will make lifelong friends. You will be bound to them with new and wonderful ties, for you will escape disaster together and you will commence shoulder to shoulder your common journey. Then you will know what it means to give of yourself that others may survive and rediscover life. You will learn the full meaning of "Love thy neighbor as thyself."

It may seem incredible that these people are to become happy, respected, and useful once more. How can they rise out of such misery, bad repute and hopelessness? The practical answer is that since these things have happened among us, they can happen with you. Should you wish them above all else, and be willing to make use of our experience, we are sure they will come. A wonderful life is still ahead of us. Our own recovery proves that!

Commentary: The original text is, "The age of miracles is still with us. Our own recovery proves that!" Webster defines a miracle as: 1- an event or action that apparently contradicts known scientific laws and is, hence, thought to be due to supernatural causes, esp. to an act of God. 2-a remarkable thing or event. 3-a wonderful example. Many members of AA agree with the first definition as the one that applies to them. Remember that we should allow every person their opinion. I prefer a more loose definition. I do believe my sobriety is a "remarkable thing or event." To believe that I am a "wonderful example" is far too egotistical for me. Sometimes I am. Sometimes I'm just a wonderfully bad example. So, feel free to choose your definition. I'm a miracle! You're a miracle! We are all miracles! Everybody gets a trophy!

Our hope is that when this chip of a book is launched on the world tide of alcoholism, defeated drinkers will seize upon it, to follow its suggestions. Many, we are sure, will rise to their feet and march on. They will approach still other sick ones and fellowships of Alcoholics Anonymous may spring up in each city and hamlet, havens for those who must find a way out.

In the chapter "Helping Others," you gathered an idea of how we approach and aid others to health. Suppose now that through you several families have adopted this way of life. You will want to know more of how to proceed from that point. Perhaps the best way of treating you to a glimpse of your future will be to describe the growth of the fellowship among us. Here is a brief account:

Years ago, in 1935, one of our number made a journey to a certain western city. From a business standpoint, his trip came off badly. Had he been successful in his enterprise, he would have been set on his feet financially which, at the time, seemed vitally important. But his venture wound up in a lawsuit and bogged down completely. The proceeding was shot through with much hard feeling and controversy.

Bitterly discouraged, he found himself in a strange place, discredited and almost broke. Still physically weak, and sober but a few months, he saw that his predicament was dangerous. He wanted so much to talk with someone, but whom?

One dismal afternoon he paced a hotel lobby wondering how his bill was to be paid. At one end of the room stood a glass covered directory of local churches. Down the lobby a door opened into an attractive bar. He could see the gay crowd inside. In there he would find companionship and release. Unless he took some drinks, he might not have the courage to scrape an acquaintance and would have a lonely weekend.

Of course he couldn't drink, but why not sit hopefully at a table, a bottle of ginger ale before him? After all, had he not been sober six months now? Perhaps he could handle, say, three drinks—no more! Fear gripped him. He was on thin ice. Again it was the old, insidious insanity—that first drink. With a shiver, he turned away and walked down the lobby to the church directory. Music and gay chatter still floated to him from the bar.

But what about his responsibilities—his family and the people who would die because they would not know how to get well, ah—yes, those other alcoholics? There must be many such in this town. He would phone a minister. His sanity returned.

Selecting a church at random from the directory, he stepped into a booth and lifted the receiver.

His call to the minister led him presently to a certain resident of the town, who, though formerly able and respected, was then nearing the nadir of alcoholic despair. It was the usual situation: home in jeopardy, wife ill, children distracted, bills in arrears and standing damaged. He had a desperate desire to stop, but saw no way out, for he had earnestly tried many avenues of escape. Painfully aware of being somehow abnormal, the man did not fully realize what it meant to be alcoholic.*

When our friend related his experience, the man agreed that no amount of will power he might muster could stop his drinking for long. A spiritual experience, he conceded, was absolutely necessary, but the price seemed high upon the basis suggested. He told how he lived in constant worry about those who might find out about his alcoholism. He had, of course, the familiar alcoholic obsession that few knew of his drinking. Why, he argued, should he lose the remainder of his business, only to bring still more suffering to his family by foolishly admitting his plight to people from whom he made his livelihood? He would do anything, he said, but that.

Being intrigued, however, he invited our friend to his home. Some time later, and just as he thought he was getting control of his liquor situation, he went on a roaring bender. For him,

---

*This refers to Bill's first visit with Dr. Bob. These men later became co-founders of A.A. Bill's story opens the text of this book; Dr. Bob's heads the Story Section

this was the spree that ended all sprees. He saw that he would have to face his problems squarely.

One morning he took the bull by the horns and set out to tell those he feared what his trouble had been. He found himself surprisingly well received, and learned that many knew of his drinking. Stepping into his car, he made the rounds of people he had hurt. He trembled as he went about, for this might mean ruin, particularly to a person in his line of business.

At midnight he came home exhausted, but very happy. He has not had a drink since. As we shall see, he now means a great deal to his community, and the major liabilities of thirty years of hard drinking have been repaired in four.

But life was not easy for the two friends. Plenty of difficulties presented themselves. Both saw that they must keep spiritually active. One day they called up the head nurse of a local hospital. They explained their need and inquired if she had a first class alcoholic prospect.

She replied, "Yes, we've got a corker. He's just beaten up a couple of nurses. Goes off his head completely when he's drinking. But he's a grand chap when he's sober, though he's been in here eight times in the last six months. Understand he was once a well-known lawyer in town, but just now we've got him strapped down tight."*

Here was a prospect all right but, by the description, none too

---

*This refers to Bill's and Dr. Bob's first visit to A.A. Number Three. See the Pioneer Section. This resulted in A.A.'s first group, at Akron, Ohio, in 1935.

promising. The use of spiritual principles in such cases was not so well understood as it is now. But one of the friends said, "Put him in a private room. We'll be down."

Two days later, a future fellow of Alcoholics Anonymous stared glassily at the strangers beside his bed. "Who are you fellows, and why this private room? I was always in a ward before."

Said one of the visitors, "We're giving you a treatment for alcoholism."

Hopelessness was written large on the man's face as he replied, "Oh, but that's no use. Nothing would fix me. I'm a goner. The last three times, I got drunk on the way home from here. I'm afraid to go out the door. I can't understand it."

For an hour, the two friends told him about their drinking experiences. Over and over, he would say: "That's me. That's me. I drink like that."

The man in the bed was told of the acute poisoning from which he suffered, how it deteriorates the body of an alcoholic and warps his mind. There was much talk about the mental state preceding the first drink.

"Yes, that's me," said the sick man, "the very image. You fellows know your stuff all right, but I don't see what good it'll do. You fellows are somebody. I was once, but I'm a nobody now. From what you tell me, I know more than ever I can't stop." At this both the visitors burst into a laugh. Said the future Fellow Anonymous: "Damn little to laugh about that I can see."

The two friends spoke of their spiritual experience and told him about the course of action they carried out.

He interrupted: "I used to be strong for the church, but that won't fix it. I've prayed to god on hangover mornings and sworn that I'd never touch another drop but by nine o'clock I'd be boiled as an owl."

Next day found the prospect more receptive. He had been thinking it over. "Maybe you're right," he said. "God ought to be able to do anything." Then he added, "He sure didn't do much for me when I was trying to fight this booze racket alone."

On the third day the lawyer gave his life to the care and direction of his higher power, and said he was perfectly willing to do anything necessary. His wife came, scarcely daring to be hopeful, though she thought she saw something different about her husband already. He had begun to have a spiritual experience.

That afternoon he put on his clothes and walked from the hospital a free man. He entered a political campaign, making speeches, frequenting gathering places of all sorts, often staying up all night. He lost the race by only a narrow margin. But he had found a power greater than himself—and in finding that, he had found himself.

That was in June, 1935. He never drank again. He too, has become a respected and useful member of his community. He has helped other people recover, and is a power in the church from which he was long absent.

So, you see, there were three alcoholics in that town, who now felt they had to give to others what they had found, or be sunk. After several failures to find others, a fourth turned up. He came through an acquaintance who had heard the good news. He proved to be a devil-may-care young fellow whose parents could not make out whether he wanted to stop drinking or not. They were deeply religious people, much shocked by their son's refusal to have anything to do with the church. He suffered horribly from his sprees, but it seemed as if nothing could be done for him. He consented, however, to go to the hospital, where he occupied the very room recently vacated by the lawyer.

He had three visitors. After a bit, he said, "The way you fellows put this spiritual stuff makes sense. I'm ready to do business. I guess the old folks were right after all." So one more was added to the Fellowship.

All this time our friend of the hotel lobby incident remained in that town. He was there three months. He now returned home, leaving behind his first acquaintance, the lawyer and the devil-may-care chap. These men had found something brand new in life. Though they knew they must help other alcoholics if they would remain sober, that motive became secondary. It was transcended by the happiness they found in giving themselves for others. They shared their homes, their slender resources, and gladly devoted their spare hours to fellow-sufferers. They were willing, by day or night, to place a new person in the hospital and visit them afterward. They grew in numbers. They experienced a few distressing failures, but in those cases they made an effort to bring the person's family into a spiritual way of living, thus relieving much worry and suffering.

A year and six months later these three had succeeded with seven more. Seeing much of each other, scarce an evening passed that someone's home did not shelter a little gathering of men and women, happy in their release, and constantly thinking how they might present their discovery to some newcomer. In addition to these casual get-togethers, it became customary to set apart one night a week for a meeting to be attended by anyone or everyone interested in a spiritual way of life. Aside from fellowship and sociability, the prime object was to provide a time and place where new people might bring their problems.

Outsiders became interested. One man and woman placed their large home at the disposal of this strangely assorted crowd. This couple has since become so fascinated that they have dedicated their home to the work. Many a distracted spouse has visited this house to find loving and understanding companionship among people who knew their problem, to hear from the lips of their spouses what had happened to them, to be advised how their own wayward mate might be hospitalized and approached when next they stumbled.

Many people, yet dazed from their hospital experience, have stepped over the threshold of that home into freedom. Many an alcoholic who entered there came away with an answer. They succumbed to that gay crowd inside, who laughed at their own misfortunes and understood theirs. Impressed by those who visited them at the hospital, they capitulated entirely when, later, in an upper room of this house, they heard the story of some person whose experience closely tallied with their own. The expression on the faces of the women, that indefinable something in the eyes of the men, the stimulating and electric atmosphere of the place, conspired to let them know that here was haven at last.

The very practical approach to their problems, the absence of intolerance of any kind, the informality, the genuine democracy, the uncanny understanding which these people had were irresistible. They would leave elated by the thought of what they could now do for some stricken acquaintance and their family. They knew they had a host of new friends; it seemed they had known these strangers always. They had seen great things, and this was to come to them. They had visioned the great reality—their higher power of fellowship, love and kindness.

*Commentary: "the absence of intolerance of any kind." It is my great hope to see tolerance re-established in AA. AA's blindness to the intolerance for secular people is a huge spiritual failing. Yes, I'm being judgmental. There are so many references in Alcoholics Anonymous regarding acceptance of all who wish to seek sobriety. When people are in favor of pounding on a belief in god as the only cornerstone for sobriety, it is nothing more than willful ignorance born of fear. Alcohol abuse kills about 20,000 people in the U.S. each year. The number is 2.5 million worldwide. Reaching **all** who suffer from alcoholism, including secular people, is not just the right thing to do. It saves lives, too. When AA disregards any portion or group of alcoholics, it is deadly. That is nothing less than hateful and barbaric. There is nothing spiritual about exclusion and intolerance. If you believe in god and are thinking, "How dare that heathen bastard preach to me about spirituality!" My response is* *this. I dare to speak truth to ugliness perpetrated in the name of god or for any other reason. I'm not afraid of anyone that claims a spiritual life but does evil, ugly and hateful things. My higher power is love. Welcoming, including and accepting all alcoholics, regardless of personal beliefs, without demanding they convert to a belief in gods, is the loving thing to do. That's how I dare.*

Now, this house will hardly accommodate its weekly visitors, for they number sixty or eighty as a rule. Alcoholics are being attracted from far and near. From surrounding towns, families drive long distances to be present. A community thirty miles away has fifteen members of Alcoholics Anonymous. Being a large place, we think that some day its Fellowship will number many hundreds.*

But life among Alcoholics Anonymous is more than attending gatherings and visiting hospitals. Cleaning up old scrapes, helping to settle family differences, explaining the disinherited son or daughter to their irate parents, lending money and securing jobs for each other, when justified—these are everyday occurrences. No one is too discredited or has sunk too low to be welcomed cordially—if they mean business. Social distinctions, petty rivalries and jealousies—these are laughed out of countenance. Being wrecked in the same vessel, being restored and united, with hearts and minds attuned to the welfare of others, the things which matter so much to some people no longer signify much to them. How could they?

Commentary: The original text is, "being restored and united under one God." This is a contradiction of "higher power as you

*Written In 1939

*understand Him." Even "as you understand **Him**" is a contradiction of the concept of allowing each AA member their own higher power. With these words, the choice of your own higher power has been further narrowed to no choice at all. I'm sure many deists, from the common AA member to the top of AA's hierarchy, see my comments here as nothing short of heresy. That's one of the problems I've had with religion throughout my life. It closes your mind to all other options and opinions. A closed mind is the cornerstone of most of the ugliness in this world.*

Under only slightly different conditions, the same thing is taking place in many eastern cities. In one of these there is a well-known hospital for the treatment of alcoholic and drug addiction. Six years ago one of our number was a patient there. We are greatly indebted to the doctor in attendance there, for he, although it might prejudice his own work, has told us of his belief in ours.

Every few days this doctor suggests our approach to one of his patients. Understanding our work, he can do this with an eye to selecting those who are willing and able to recover on a spiritual basis. Many of us, former patients, go there to help. Then, in this eastern city, there are informal meetings such as we have described to you, where you may now see scores of members. There are the same fast friendships, there is the same helpfulness to one another as you find among our western friends. There is a good bit of travel between East and West and we foresee a great increase in this helpful interchange.

Some day we hope that every alcoholic who journeys will find a Fellowship of Alcoholics Anonymous at their destination. To some extent this is already true. Some of us are salespeople and go about. Little clusters of twos and threes and fives of us have sprung up in other communities, through contact with our two larger centers. Those of us who travel drop in as often as we can. This practice enables us to lend a hand, at the same time avoiding certain alluring distractions of the road, about which any traveling person can inform you.*

Thus we grow. And so can you, though you be but one person with this book in your hand. We believe and hope it contains all you will need to begin.

We know what you are thinking. You are saying to yourself: "I'm jittery and alone. I couldn't do that." But you can. You forget that you have just now tapped a source of power much greater than yourself. To duplicate, with such backing, what we have accomplished is only a matter of willingness, patience and labor.

We know of an A.A. member who was living in a large community. They had lived there but a few weeks when they found that the place probably contained more alcoholics per square mile than any city in the country. This was only a few days ago at this writing. (1939) The authorities were much concerned. This person got in touch with a prominent psychiatrist who had undertaken certain responsibilities for the mental health of the community. The doctor proved to be able and exceedingly anxious to adopt any workable method of

---

*Written in 1939. In 2012, there are over 108,000 groups. There is A.A. activity in approximately 170 countries, with an estimated membership of over two million.

handling the situation. So the doctor inquired, what did our friend have on the ball?

Our friend proceeded to tell them. And with such good effect that the doctor agreed to a test among their patients and certain other alcoholics from a clinic which they attend. Arrangements were also made with the chief psychiatrist of a large public hospital to select still others from the stream of misery which flows through that institution.

So our member will soon have friends galore. Some of them may sink and perhaps never get up, but if our experience is a criterion, more than half of those approached will become members of Alcoholics Anonymous. When a few people in this city have found themselves, and have discovered the joy of helping others to face life again, there will be no stopping until everyone in that town has had their opportunity to recover—if they can and will.

Still you may say: "But I will not have the benefit of contact with you who write this book." We cannot be sure. You must remember that your real reliance is always upon fellowship and a power greater than yourself. With determination you can create the fellowship you crave.*

Our book is meant to be suggestive only. We realize we know only a little. Advancements in science and knowledge will constantly disclose more to you and to us. Seek answers in your morning meditation what you can do each day for the

---

*Alcoholics Anonymous will be glad to hear from you. Address P.O. Box 459, Grand Central Station, New York, NY 10163.

person who is still sick. The answers will come, if your own house is in order. But obviously you cannot transmit something you haven't got. See to it that your relationship with your higher power is right, and great events will come to pass for you and countless others. This is the great fact for us.

Commentary: The first two sentences of this paragraph (unchanged from the Fourth Edition) is acknowledgment that the Big Book should not be taken as dogma. This is the author's humble statement that alcoholics should look to the future knowing that more about addiction and alcoholism will be learned. Science has added much to our present understanding and it will continue to do so. The original text says that god will disclose this information but, as far as I can tell, god ain't talking.

Abandon yourself to your higher power as you understand it. Admit your faults to yourself and to others. Clear away the wreckage of your past. Give freely of what you find and join us. We shall share fellowship with you in spirit, and you will surely meet some of us as you trudge the road of happy destiny.

May the fellowship of AA and love embrace you—until then.

Stories And Appendices

The first 164 pages of the Big Book are only the beginning. Although it is the heart of the AA program, there is much more to be said about the rest of the Big Book. The page numbers I mention now are referencing those of *Alcoholics Anonymous* (Fourth Edition).

On page 165 the personal stories begin. Personal stories are just that ... personal ... and should not be changed. I might disagree with certain opinions in the stories, but those opinions should be respected just as I wish mine to be. However, I will comment on some of them. Also, I take exception when the author gets preachy. Watch for an abundance of the "I" pronoun. That's a sure sign the author is speaking about themselves. When they start using you, us, we, etc., it might be the time to open your eyes and see the proselytizing. This advice should be used while reading my book, also. Everybody, including myself, is afflicted with the desire to get preachy at times. Also, *Alcoholics Anonymous* gives a brief description at the beginning of each story. That, of course, is no more than commentary and subject to criticism.

I have always been curious about who these people are and how their stories were included in these various editions of *Alcoholics Anonymous*. They seem like ordinary folks. A good cross section of the membership one might think. Well, that's sort of correct. At least the editors made an attempt at making it appear that way. There is a black guy. There is a gay person. There is, even, an agnostic. Or, at least, it was someone who had a brush with agnosticism. He is, what one might call, an ambiguous agnostic. I'm not saying there is bias in the choosing of these stories, but (okay, I am saying) if you would like your story included in the next edition, I would advise that a profound religious conversion is your best bet. A good "God" punch line at the end of your story wouldn't hurt, either. Actually, I had one of those once. Remember that I was told to add an "o" to the word "god" so it would become "good." While I was in my desperation to find sound sobriety and before I decided I didn't need a god, I would say, "I never found good until I found god." The crowd loved it! They ate it up! Applause for the converted atheist was enthusiastically given. That would be a good line to use on the editors of the next edition. Oh … yeah … wait … maybe I just spoiled that. Oh, well. I'm going to take a wild-assed guess here and say I probably will never get my story in that book anyway.

On page 180, Dr. Bob mentions the "spiritual approach." This is one of the keys to sobriety for so many alcoholics including many secular ones. Dr. Bob and other pioneers of AA had no idea that this spiritual approach could be made without a belief in a supernatural being. The meaning of the term has evolved since then. Today, I understand this to be not just religious, but goodness, kindness, love, virtue, awe, etc. The old meaning was being of the spirits or soul and not human. I like the natural definition of it. I understand it as my attempt to refine myself. Both definitions disregard material matters. The heart of it goes to the pursuit and practice of personal betterment.

On page 181, Dr. Bob turns from his story (using "I") to

address the reader (using "you"). Describing atheism, agnosticism and skepticism as a form of intellectual pride is little more than propaganda for religious promotion. Drawing a parallel, one might describe illiteracy pride. The inverse idea might be intellectual denial. It suggests that religion, especially one's own religion, is infallible. Religious people refer to intellectual pride as something negative, arrogant and self-righteous. They say it should be avoided as sinful. This is nothing more than religious rhetoric. It is an attack on critical independent thinking. The successful promotion of religious ideas requires this repudiation of thinkers. Espousing anti-intellectualism has been the tool of religion, dictators and politicians for centuries. Keeping the masses ignorant is the easiest way to control them. Shrug this idea off like an old, ragged coat. Also, I avoid AA members that say, "Don't think, don't drink, and go to meetings." Accepting that notion is the first step into dogmatism. Also, I will be eternally confused by AA's slogan "Think Think Think." Are they reminding themselves that thinking is, really, a good thing or are they making fun of thinking? I grin every time I see it.

While I am very grateful for all the world's intellectualism, there are plenty of intellectuals that are self-righteous and arrogant, too. There are good and bad people everywhere you look. Intellectualism is what fuels society's growth. I don't claim to be an intellectual, but if I was, I would want to be the kind of intellectual that constantly questions everything and everyone, including myself and my own ideas. Embrace your intellect, but also develop the ability to think past your own rhetoric and nonsense. I try to remember that I lie to myself more than anyone else. We may not want others to tell us what to think, but be sure to not let yourself close the door to new thinking. I have no doubt that I am my own worst enemy. One of my best assets is knowing that I can't figure all this out on my own. I listen to every idea and carefully decide what is right (for me). My own critical thinking is good. Fortunately, it's just a part of a much larger mass of critical thinking. This huge library of thought is a wonderful asset that we can use to develop our own ideas about life as we choose to live it. So, Dr. Bob, please don't feel sorry for me. I'm very proud of my intellect.

On page 208, the editor comments, "Who am I to say there is no God?" I am me! I'm the guy that doesn't give my thinking over to anyone else. This is a great example of using "intellectual pride" as a weapon against critical thinking.

On page 232, is "Jim's Story." It is new to the "Pioneers of AA" section. Part of what it describes is the separation of races within AA. I wouldn't expect much less regarding this in the '30s and '40s. In fact, during those decades, black people were not allowed to attend AA meetings in most places. I have read accounts regarding house meetings of this period. If black people were allowed to be present, they had to stay in the kitchen while the meeting was being conducted in the living room. Also, they could only drink their coffee from broken cups. This was done so that a white person wouldn't make the horrible mistake of drinking from a cup that had been used by a black person. Much has been accomplished regarding the worst kinds of racism in AA. Apparently, subtle racism still lingers in 2001. The authors of the commentary before the story choose to use the term "his people." Every day I strive to grow beyond the notions of "them" or "others." I want to embrace the idea that there are no "others." Black people overcame this segregation by insisting that racism and discrimination were spiritual issues. Spiritual principles must take precedence over personalities, politics, faith, fear and ignorance. I believe the struggles that black people endured are good lessons for the secular community within AA as we struggle for acceptance and inclusion.

On page 279, is a very good commentary on today's alcoholic. When I first came to AA in 1980, I knew people that carried a bottle of whiskey in the trunk of their car. If you went on a 12 step call, you wanted to be sure you could deal with a person going into DTs. I had a friend going into DTs in my kitchen. I poured whiskey into his coffee to stop it. Ah, the good old days! Ha! They, really, were the bad old days. Delirium tremens are almost unheard of today. There is ample opportunity to get dry under controlled conditions monitored by medical staff. I don't always agree with the recovery industry, but it does have some benefits. The advent of numerous treatment centers and half-way houses have created a lot of awareness of addiction and the problems created by it. I was 30 when I first went to an AA meeting. In the early years of my sobriety, I was surprised to see anyone younger than 25. Today, I'm seeing teenagers coming into AA. That is a very good thing.

In the middle of page 287, this person says he came to AA as an agnostic and later found God. He says that he was new to "the idea that religion and spirituality were not one and the same." This is the cornerstone that my AA beliefs are built upon. Anyone can use the AA program, find spirituality and stay sober, regardless of a belief or lack of a belief in a supernatural being. "Our only wish is to assure suffering alcoholics that they can achieve sobriety with the support of AA without having to accept anyone else's beliefs or having to deny their own."

On page 301, I find it rather quaint that a physician could, finally, realize "that God, not he, was the Great Healer." But, the title is "Physician, Heal Thyself." So, which way are we going here—make up your mind, editor. I know this may be frivolous negativity. Sometimes, my smartassedness gets in my way. I apologize. "When you are wrong, promptly admit it." Hey! I'm a wonderful example!

On page 369, the editors' short description says, "A barrier to God collapsed." That suggests the person is no longer agnostic. I'm not so sure of that. I suppose it could be argued both ways. In the story, upper case letters are used for higher power. Did the author do that or did that happen in editing by AA World Services? On page 374, it reads, "Having such an experience didn't lead me to any certainty about God." I don't know if this person is just being purposely ambiguous or if AA is just planting the suggestion of belief in a deity to make the inclusion of an agnostic's story more palatable. It seems like a kind of sleight-of-hand. With one hand, AA gives us a story about an agnostic. With the other hand they take it away. The value of this story, for me, disappears like magic!

On page 374, the author of this story says, "Alcoholics Anonymous gives me the freedom to believe and to doubt as much as I need to." That may or may not be AA's official position, but I would love to know what meetings this person goes to. My experience was different. Usually, AA members aren't so generous, understanding and accepting enough to give me that freedom. I must claim it for myself. And, most AA members don't care to hear from those that express this freedom. If you don't believe in God, you might be considered a second-class member by some in AA. Perhaps third- or fourth-class behind people of color and gays that do believe in God. Prejudice of any kind has no place in a *spiritual* program.

In the middle of page 406, is the loathsome idea of a Jew being told they should accept "The Lord's Prayer" out of gratitude. Let's try to ignore that and focus on this person's idea about the difference between religion and spirituality. Our Jewish friend has a fairly decent idea here in that spirituality is how we feel about what we do. This is a good jumping-off point. We should go deeper, but it's a good beginning. Mazel tov!

When someone says, "We don't talk about drugs here" or "This is AA and all we talk about is alcohol," ask them to read the story on page 407.

With three strikes against her (poor, black and alcoholic) the Big Book editors' comments on page 531 say, "She felt shut away from any life worth living." Why do they include being black in there? The woman never makes any kind of comment like that in her story. Well, I think I know why. It's because far too many white people know how poorly they think of and treat black people. With that perspective, it's quite easy to believe being black is, at best, a burden. Regardless of what the authors were thinking, it was a negative and ugly thing to say. It can't be read any other way. Actually, I don't believe the editors were thinking at all.

On page 534, are comments by a black woman about black people staying away from AA. It's all so true and pathetic. This is very significant and telling about AA. Alcoholics Anonymous claims to have a "big tent." Unfortunately, my friends, that is untrue. I believe this problem is improving every day, but AA has a long way to go.

On page 553, the editors' comment is, "we have to deal with sobriety every day." This is a bit of a nugget. Every solution creates another problem. This is so true with sobriety. If you don't drink, you solve the drinking problem. But, now you have a new problem. How shall we live without alcohol? Stopping drinking is not the key to sobriety. How you live sober is the key. You can do nothing and hate sobriety or you can change and love it.

So, here we are at the end of the stories. I have my thoughts about the stories in general, but I will share some thoughts about a few in particular. We have an African-American that addresses the "black problem" in AA, but dismisses it as foolishness by black alcoholics. We have a Jew that agrees to be grateful for the honor of listening to a Christian prayer. We have an agnostic that seems to be leaning towards belief in a supernatural being. And, we have a gay person starting the first gay group in his area. These stories seem to me to be too neat and tidy. These are minorities in AA that not only say they don't experience any prejudice in AA, but they agree that the white Christian way is the right way. Sometimes I question the validity of these stories' authorship. At the very least, the people that select stories for inclusion in the Big Book only select stories that support AA's biased perspective. Everybody has some bias. Spiritual principles dictate that we attempt to recognize these defects of character and correct our behavior, so as to act in a more loving way. I hope that, one day, the organization of AA and the membership will recognize this bias and how it perpetuates discrimination towards the minority members of Alcoholics Anonymous.

The truth is this. Black, gay, non-Christian and secular alcoholics stay away from "regular" AA for a good reason. They are not welcomed like white, straight, Christian and other god-loving people. A white Christian man with 51 years of sobriety recently told me that these people have their own meetings because they "just want to be different." That comment is no more than a poor excuse to support and perpetuate the very unspiritual thinking and behavior that is racism, homophobia, sectarianism, hate, fear and discrimination. We're not different because we "just want to be." We're different because **we are** different. Black people can't be white. Gay people can't be straight, although they may be bisexual or curious. Secular people can't be theists, although some might change their minds.

Nonetheless, minorities wish to be accepted, respected and included as **they are** in "regular" AA because, when it comes to alcoholism, we are all the same. The fact that these people feel the need to have separate meetings is because of this lack of understanding, respect and acceptance in "regular" AA.

They don't feel welcome at "regular" AA meetings. I'm sure "regular" AA members will deny this because many are unaware of their disrespect and unwelcoming manner. They have little idea about how to be truly inclusive. Minorities, on the other hand, are very aware of this behavior and the Big Book's biased text. And then, they wonder why we reject AA and its literature.

This is a spiritual failing of AA and its members. Alcoholics Anonymous, as an organization, needs to clearly and emphatically reject this engrained discrimination that has flourished since the beginning. My great fear is that, someday, AA will find itself on the wrong side of history. This new spiritual position and directive must come from the very top of AA. Many individual AA members understand the spiritual principles of acceptance, inclusion, respect and love for every member regardless of who they are or what they believe. A large portion of AA's membership does not understand this and will not change until it is a directive from the AA "mountain top." Even then, some members will never accept minorities. That is their problem to resolve or not. Please AA, for the sake of all alcoholics and the organization itself, find the spiritual high road. Giving up your stranglehold on the Christian thing might seem like the wrong decision, but in the end that tight grip will only suffocate AA.

On page 561, we have the Traditions. What is this AA unity Tradition One speaks of? Is it real unity with every person regardless of color, religion, sexuality, deity or lack of a belief in deities being equal, welcome and accepted wholeheartedly in the rooms of AA? It doesn't seem to speak to that kind of unity. It seems to be just white Christian unity. Am I wrong? Okay, good! I really, truly and honestly want to be wrong about this. But, don't just tell me I'm wrong. Show me. I challenge every member of AA to show me true unity. Show me through your actions. Show me through your friendship. Show me through your respect. I would love that so much! The spiritual option is to accept diversity and equality with open arms or, at least admit that you are wrong and try to change. The unspiritual option is to readjust your blinders and enjoy the comfort of being with only those people that look and think like you do.

In Tradition Two, I would replace "a loving God as He may express Himself" with "spiritual principles as expressed in our group conscience." I can hear it now. "OMG! You can't change the Traditions!" Well, yes, you can. As written, my higher power as *I* understand it is being changed to the group's understanding. This may seem very democratic for the group's purposes. Unfortunately, it creates a very narrow understanding for the newcomer that shows up at the group. This notion of sanctioned discrimination against all that don't hold the beliefs of the group is divisive and repelling newcomer alcoholics by the thousands. If AA wants to grow and help all these alcoholics, it must wholeheartedly accept diversity. I believe diversity will someday come to AA, whether AA likes it or not. The only question that remains is, do you want to be bulldozed into it or would you prefer to take the spiritual high road and be the organization that you claim to be for *all* of your members?

Traditions Three, Four and Five explain that spiritual high road very well. And, I'll say this to the trustees of AA's General Service Board. Please try to place the spiritual principles of inclusion and acceptance before your Christian personalities. Remember, "***Universal** respect is the key to your usefulness*" (Tradition 9-The Long Form). It will be okay ... honest. God will love you for it.

Tradition 10 (long form) states, "No AA group or member should ever, in such a way as to implicate AA, express an opinion on outside controversial issues—particularly those of politics, alcohol reform, or sectarian religion." For anyone that thinks I'm breaking Traditions, keep in mind that I'm expressing my opinion on *internal* controversial issues. Sectarianism has no place inside AA. But that is, exactly, what has been happening since the beginning of AA. The favoritism towards Christianity is not only real, but blatant and pervasive worldwide. Yes, it's worldwide. In countries where Christianity is unusual, Christian AA members act like missionaries. AA never claims to be religious, but it acts like a religion. It's becoming this new religion with Christianity as its cornerstone. As the majority, Christian AA members eat this up with little or no regard for minority beliefs. This is what is known as the "arrogance of the majority." Also, keep in mind that if I am breaking Traditions, I feel it must be done. This problem is, in my opinion, far more important than a transgression against AA Traditions. The longer this discrimination continues, the more it will threaten the integrity of Alcoholics Anonymous. Resolving this problem is crucial for AA's strong and continued success.

Now we are at Appendix II on Page 567. With only a few

exceptions, I think this explanation of a "Spiritual Experience" is very good. It addresses the profound change of thinking that was needed for me to embrace a life of sobriety. As much as I don't care for the term "spiritual," it is becoming less of a reference to supernatural things. It is often used today to mean virtuous, or of the human spirit, or intellect and a refinement of thoughts and feelings. It's the awe I feel while viewing a beautiful sunrise. Some believe things like karma or a connectedness to nature are considered spiritual. Spirituality (for me) is that connection I have with my better self. My better self is that person I wish to be. It's the virtues of love, kindness and empathy that I express to other people and the natural world around me. It's a sense of grace within me that makes me feel good about myself. Because it is such an exceptional term, I find it to be a difficult word to replace. I try to keep in mind that this is 80-year-old thinking the authors of the Big Book are using. Forgive them and put your 21st century spin on it. Many times the authors use "spiritual" and "religious" as interchangeable. To religious people, they are. We think otherwise. Over and over, you will see the terms spiritual, spiritual life, spiritual remedy, spiritual answer, etc. Understand that, for secular people, it means virtue or a similar concept of graciousness. You know ... things like love, empathy, generosity and kindness, or anything you wish it to mean for yourself. The essence of what I'm trying to say is, make it work for you instead of allowing it to be a problem on your journey through sobriety.

At the bottom of page 568, you will find the often heard "contempt prior to investigation." Investigating AA and the Big Book are difficult at best. Especially if you can't read past or around all the religious references and the word "God." That is my purpose in writing this book. Far too many secular alcoholics refuse to read AA's Big Book. They reject AA's fellowship and program because of a contempt even after their investigation. I'm not suggesting that AA is for everyone. But, it did work for this atheist.

AA has never updated "The Medical View On A.A." on page 569. Look at the dates here. The latest is 1949. This "Medical View" is really just a few medical doctors and psychiatrists offering nothing more than opinions. There is no science here. It is not even an overall medical view. So the question must be asked: Why doesn't AA update this? There is some peer-reviewed science that suggests that AA's methodology works. Doctors specializing in addictions understand that addictive drugs (including alcohol) act on the mid-brain to increase the need for a higher than normal level of dopamine and prevents the prefrontal cortex (the thinking part of the brain) from working properly. Abstinence calms the mid-brain and personal growth strengthens the cortex. With fellowship to support these efforts, we have AA's trifecta for successful recovery. All this enhances one's probability of long-term sobriety. There now are many scientific studies regarding alcoholism and drug addiction. I believe AA should be a primary source for current scientific information regarding addiction and recovery. AA should, at the least, direct its members to these studies.

Quantifying AA's success rate is another matter and nearly impossible. In 2014, there was a study titled "Estimating the Efficacy of Alcoholics Anonymous without Self-Selection Bias:

An Instrumental Variables Re-Analysis of Randomized Clinical Trials" which was published by the International Society for Biomedical Research on Alcoholism and funded by VA Health Services and the National Institute on Alcohol Abuse and Alcoholism. Its conclusion: "For most individuals seeking help for alcohol problems, increasing AA attendance leads to short- and long-term decreases in alcohol consumption that cannot be attributed to self-selection. However, for populations with high pre-existing AA involvement, further increases in AA attendance may have little impact." The term "self-selection" in the study refers to people in one control group moving to another control group. The limitations of all studies are widely acknowledged. Obtaining accurate data is very difficult because controlling the people within the study group is next to impossible. Not being able to control others … where have I heard that before?

Over the years, I've heard all sorts of numbers thrown around regarding AA's success rate. My personal feeling (very scientific, right?) is that it's about 5-15%. I have also heard that AA has its own numbers indicating that, after 6 months, only 7% of new attendees remain in the program. In my research, I have not been able to find any success rate given by AA. I'll admit that I didn't spend countless hours looking for it. Regardless, whatever the number is, it's quite low. To be sure, other methods used for sobriety don't indicate any better outcomes. Short-term rehabilitation programs are happy to tell us they have a success rate of 70-80%. Unfortunately they have no reliable way of tracking their clients after they leave these residential programs. If I had a program that held you prisoner, I could guarantee a 100% success rate while in my custody. All these figures are quite useless. If AA was a pharmaceutical drug, the FDA would never approve it. Nevertheless, I'm extremely grateful to be in the small minority. Also, this may be a good time to point out that AA will not keep you sober … **you will.** It is very clear that what **you do** to stay sober is the most important factor.

In Appendix V, we get the religious view on AA. This isn't all religions. It's just the Christian view. Is it any great surprise that the Christian community supports AA? I wonder what the Pastafarian view is? Maybe the next edition of the Big Book should include "The Secular View On AA." Maybe that's what my book is. No, actually my book is just a small contribution to the secular view. As we progress, the secular view is being heard more and more. As it should be, this secular view encompasses a very large variety of opinion. It is very heartwarming to see secular AA members coming out from the shadows and becoming a significant voice within the AA community. The days of being quiet and fitting in are over for many, if not most, of us. Together we can encourage more secular members to step out from those shadows and into the light. Hmmm … "step into the light" has a bit of a religious note to it. Oh, well … it sounds good to me. I'm leaving it.

On page 574, are the Twelve Concepts. These are directives for AA's service structure. As governing ideas, I believe they are a very good guideline. I do, however, believe that AA is far too democratic. Concept V creates a "Right of Appeal" so the minority opinion may be heard. Unfortunately, there is no concept that creates "Equal Rights." That is why minorities struggle for inclusion in AA. The "arrogance of the majority" prevails and creates a kind of second class membership for those not in the majority.

Nonetheless, I feel it is important to get involved in the business of AA. We have little choice but to accept this system of governance and work within it for change. If you can, become a GSR for your home group. The more secular voices heard means we will have greater influence.

Service in AA is like the third leg of the stool. Giving back to AA and other members is a big part of how most of us stay sober. It's understandable that many will not want to get involved with the politics of AA.

Sharing your experience, strength and hope at a meeting or one-on-one with another alcoholic is a great way to give back. In the beginning of my sobriety, all I could offer was setting up chairs and making coffee. Help to clean up after the meeting. If you are asked to chair a meeting or speak at a meeting, try your very best to accept the invitation.

Whatever it is that you can do to serve other alcoholics will always be a greater benefit to yourself. Maybe the coffee will be too strong or weak. Maybe you'll stumble and stammer throughout your talk at a speaker meeting. None of this matters. We are not professional baristas or speakers. What's important is that these things will help you stay sober. Being a "giver" is one of the best ways of feeling good about yourself. If you refuse any type of service work, the only one you will let down is yourself.

Conclusion

This book is, essentially, about change. In it, I have challenged AA as an organization to change. That, I believe, is critical to the future health and well-being of Alcoholics Anonymous. I won't carry on any further about what changes need to be made. If AA's leaders read this book, they will already know my opinion. Also, my opinion may be much more than they care to hear. I understand that my opinion is just one of many. It is very difficult to hear criticism objectively. Hopefully, some religious members of AA will read this and give it consideration. The continued failure of AA to recognize the reality of all alcoholics and their diverse beliefs is a major spiritual failing. Alcoholics Anonymous is a great organization, but this blindness limits what AA could be.

Alcoholics Anonymous is a very democratic organization. To a great degree it is ruled by its members. Unfortunately, majority rule within AA is so powerful that it is used to silence and exclude minority opinion and concerns. It is used to justify a lack of empathy for minorities. Minority groups within AA have no protections from the arrogance of the majority. I fear this discrimination, prejudice and selfishness will be tolerated to the point of AA's eminent collapse. I hope I am very wrong.

You and I have no time to wait out this folly. We cannot wait for AA to find a path of acceptance for who we are. We must find our own path to sobriety now. If you choose Alcoholics Anonymous as your method for sobriety, this book may help you to navigate it. Positive change within ourselves is critical for any long-term sobriety.

Fellowship and personal change are what I believe is most important to me and the greater focus of my sobriety. I hope I have shown secular people a way to use AA and the book *Alcoholics Anonymous* in a way that makes better sense for them. We do not have to reinvent the wheel. We do, however, need to understand that the secular path to sobriety is one of the integral spokes of the AA wheel. They are not all Christian spokes. Some are. There are, also Black, Hispanic, Asian, gay, Jewish, Muslim, Buddhist, agnostic, atheist and a large variety of other spokes that make up that wheel. After getting onto the outer rim of the wheel, you may choose any spoke you wish to travel to the hub of sobriety, serenity, love and joy! Like those old merry-go-rounds of playgrounds past, being in the center is a more stable ride.

I emphasized love as a power greater than myself because that is what my higher power is. I use it only because that is what I know. If you want a higher power, you should discover your own. One bit of advice regarding higher powers that I am extremely confident in giving is that it is **_not_** a door knob or a light bulb. Here, I can refer you back to the Big Book, page 50, second paragraph: *"In our personal stories you will find a wide variation in the way each teller approaches and conceives of the Power which is greater than himself. Whether we agree with a particular approach or conception seems to make little difference. Experience has taught us that these are matters about which, for our purpose, we need not be worried. They are questions for each individual to settle for himself."* With the exceptions of the use of the upper case in the word "power," and the sexist use of the word "himself," I completely agree with what the authors of *Alcoholics Anonymous* write here. Wouldn't it be nice if AA and all its' members did?

While writing this book, I received the October 2016 issue of the AA *Grapevine*. In a special section, five stories from atheist and agnostic members were included, along with a letter from a past chair of the General Service Board, Rev. Ward B. Ewing. I thoroughly enjoyed the stories. I related to so many of the experiences these people shared. One of the stories was from a gentleman (Marnin M.) that I know personally. The Episcopal priest's letter was so very inspirational. To have a member of the Christian clergy support our position is wonderful. So much of his letter parallels the ideas and thoughts I've expressed in this book. All of this gives me great hope that AA is moving in the right direction. I believe, deep in my heart, that the "spiritual principles" argument is the key to our full acceptance into the AA organization. Once the organization is on board, the members of AA that lean towards dogmatism will be more likely to follow. Maybe AA will land on the right side of history after all.

I'll leave you with two quotes from one of AA's co-founders. Actually, I hear secular AA members quoting Mr. Wilson quite often. It would behoove Alcoholics Anonymous to pay more attention to his writings and commentaries. Of course, If AA won't listen to Bill Wilson, what chance do I have?

"Simply because we have convictions that work very well for us, it becomes quite easy to assume that we have all of the truth. Whenever this brand of arrogance develops we are sure to become aggressive. We demand agreement with us. We play God. This isn't good dogma. This is very bad dogma. It could be especially destructive for us of AA to indulge in this sort of thing."

Bill Wilson, General Service Conference, 1965

"Our very first concern should be with those sufferers that we are still unable to reach. Newcomers are approaching us at the rate of tens of thousands yearly. They represent almost every belief and attitude imaginable. We have atheists and agnostics. We have people of nearly every race, culture and religion. How much and how often did we fail them?"

Bill Wilson, General Service Conference, 1965

Personal Secular Stories

This book needs to be more than a window into Alcoholics Anonymous. It, also, needs to be a mirror. The "window" part of the book is no more than my own view of AA and the book *Alcoholics Anonymous*. By sharing what I see through my window, I hope to influence others to take a look at AA for themselves. I encourage you to develop your own opinion by actively listening to all ideas. To begin your "listening," I have included these stories. They are the mirror that reflects AA's secular membership. They are a small example of who we are.

As I said earlier in the book, I have no desire or need to change anyone's story. I was extremely careful while editing these stories. I had to be certain not to change the content or meaning of what the authors wrote. The extent of my editing was, mostly, to correct spelling, grammar and punctuation. The stories were then sent back to the authors for their approval.

Here are secular alcoholics sharing their experience, strength and hope in sobriety. I hope you will see a little bit of yourself in their stories. Perhaps one or two of them will inspire you to get sober or build on the sobriety that you have. To grow as a person is the essence of sobriety. It's a beautiful world out there and all we have to do is reach for it.

At the time of this book's first printing, there were only three stories to include. This new edition has two more stories. I would like to request that you submit your story for future printings. Your story is important and somebody needs to hear it. The addition of new stories can be updated often. Please submit your story to: SecularAAstories@aol.com. Thank you.

Joy!

As a child, I attended the Anglican church and belonged to the young people's group. I taught Sunday school as a teenager and had pleasant times doing so. Later on, my brother, whom I adored, left the university in his last year to join a cult-like church that verbally attacked our family. He moved out, which was heartbreaking for me and my family.

Later on, when I was married and had kids, we were living in New Jersey and there were rumblings about blacks going to riot in our area. We didn't have minorities in our neighborhood or schools. I wanted our kids to get to know blacks in a friendly setting, so I sent them to the Baptist church where there were some blacks in attendance. My kids were friends with them and we had them over to our house. This was frowned upon by some neighbors. Later on, I was told by one of my daughters that, while attending that Sunday school, she was taught that she should only marry a Baptist! Since then, I have let myself acknowledge the inconsistencies of the message of love with the actions of hate.

When I first started going to AA meetings, I was terrified that it wouldn't work for me. It was the last resort, so I was intense on following the suggestions. I joined a home group, got a sponsor and started attending meetings daily. Sometimes, I attended two a day. I remember looking at the 12 Steps that were hanging in the front of the room ... and then I saw Step 2. Came to believe that a power greater than myself could restore me to sanity? What would that power be? Then I saw

Step 3. Turn my life over to the God of my understanding! God with a capital G! I rushed to my sponsor with my worries that this program wouldn't work for me, but she told me to use "group of drunks." I relaxed a bit and agreed. Later on, I found out that my sponsor was Catholic. "Oh, no!" "What am I going to do?" Well, I kept my sponsor and she never mentioned her religion to me. She didn't use religious terms. She stuck to the basics of the program, led me through the Steps and was there when I needed her. We were not pals. She was my guide to sobriety. She kept it simple, taught me to use slogans and was a power of example. She was a true friend. Because of her guidance, I have been sober over 37 years. She has since died and I now have a new sponsor who happens to feel, like me, that religion should be kept out of the program.

Over the years, I have tried different methods of a higher power. Sometimes a female God or a rotund, happy, monk-like fellow sharing a small tippy rowboat with me. When riding my motorcycle, which is something I took up in sobriety, I will look up and say, "It's Joy!" "I'm on the road again (just in case)." I figure if there is a God, he doesn't care if I believe in him or not. My choice of a God wouldn't have an ego problem and would chuckle at my disbelief … like a loving parent.

I don't join in with the lord's prayer, but I will say the serenity prayer. It's not important to me who I am saying it to. Maybe it's to myself. Maybe some spirit. All I know is that it calms me and reminds me that I am a member of AA and for that I am forever grateful.

Sometimes I'm envious of those who believe. For them, it's

simple: just turn it over. I'm uncomfortable in third-step meetings where so much religion is talked about, rather than spirituality. Sometimes, I share what I have tried. At other times, I keep quiet and wish I were more eloquent so that those having a problem with this subject would feel relief that they are not alone and that the program can work for them. I have heard that I will eventually "come around." I wonder when that might be! Joy ... just one of a group of drunks.

Alli O.

I could start with family history and give my theory on how and why I became an alcoholic, but that's not relevant to my story.

I drank for 25 years, maybe 20 of them alcoholically. Every day, for the last six months or so of drinking, I would wake and promise myself, "I will not drink today." Then I would quit for a day or two and then start again.

I was drunk at 8 a.m. one morning and my husband said to me, "This isn't working." I looked into his eyes and saw that I was breaking his heart and his spirit. I don't have the right to do that to another person, especially one I love. That was the turning point for me.

Fortunately, I had a friend/co-worker with recovery experience. When I talked to her about my problem, she recommended a therapist who had many patients with substance abuse issues. After only a few visits with her, I knew I was on the right path and during one visit she told me that AA was a strong recommendation to her patients, so I followed through. After a few months of three times a week of traditional meetings and once a week sessions with my therapist, I felt that I was headed in the right direction, but I had difficulty with the religious aspect and structured format of the meetings. It didn't seem right that I was making a huge effort to be honest with myself and others, but then I wasn't being true to myself by praying to a god I didn't believe in. It was hypocritical and contrary to what I was trying to accomplish.

The traditional AA meetings were suggesting I let someone else fix my problem and turn it over to something I don't even believe in. There were two problems with that. First, I believed it was my responsibility to fix the problem, and secondly, I don't believe in a supreme being. This was a waste of my time and I had already wasted 25 years.

My therapist then recommended a freethinkers meeting that was held in the town I lived in. The following week, I attended my first meeting of this We Agnostics group. Immediately, I felt accepted and at home with like-minded people. Their goals were similar to mine. They believed we were all there to get sober, stay sober and live a good sober life … not get religion.

I realized that I needed strength. My goals were to be accountable and mature. Also, to understand who and what I was and fix it. The fellowship would help me with this endeavor and then, if I didn't drink, my life would be less troublesome and more fulfilling. I know that sounds simple, and it was anything but. The alternative, though, was unacceptable.

For the past 10 years, I have been participating in this group. I have learned a lot by listening to others share. The collective wisdom of this group has led me in the right direction toward self-growth, which is my program. When I look back now, I see that that specific group of individuals was exactly who and what I needed at that time. They taught me so much and accepted me unconditionally. It worked for me. Not everyone can say that. In fact, most can't and I have no idea why this worked so well for me, but I have not had a drink since I quit on March 24, 2007.

Today, I am still me, with my fears, obsessive thoughts and behaviors. That was the only disappointment to being sober. I have learned that even though I will always be an anxious person and I will always be obsessive, I no longer feel a need to drink to ease my anxiety. Now, I find that I can identify the thoughts that trigger my unease. I am doing my best to manage these issues. So, I finally know who I am and, most days, I'm good with that. My therapist was responsible for that breakthrough. I am so grateful for her counseling and compassion.

AA has also opened my eyes and mind to many methods of dealing with life as a sober person. Each of us has something to offer to others and we learn by listening to them share their stories. A friend once said, "None of us arrived here on the wings of victory." Isn't that the truth?

The winner of this story is, of course, me. There is another winner ... maybe by collateral good fortune or maybe by my positive influence. It doesn't matter. My mother, who stopped drinking at the age of 81, is now my sober buddy in a totally alcoholic family. We understand each other and we are available for each other. I treasure our relationship.

But, what's next? What's after AA?

I don't see myself attending AA meetings forever. However, I do know that I will always be in touch with another alcoholic. I have made good and lasting friends with some members of our group. We share an understanding of an alcoholic's triumphs and failures. We are there for each other—always.

Elisabeth H.

In 1994, I realized that instead of going to Al-Anon, I belonged in AA. Aha!

I knew about a local We Agnostics meeting. This meeting is still my home group. There, friends have served as sponsors and the conversation allows for a wide range of topics, including religious ones for anyone in attendance, but God is not a focus. It is a place that does not rely on trite slogans, does not focus on egotistic sponsorship or close with prayer. Our group conscience suggests we need to personally do the work to realize a positive continuing sobriety and not turn over our will to the care of an invisible being. I had no real experience in my life with prayer, except for saying grace for food and good-night to the moon.

I did not drink as a teen and my parents drank only occasionally, until my mother's illness led her to drink sherry in the evenings. As her caregiver, I fell into drinking with her, captive to her vice in her discomfort. This felt strange to me, but I began to look forward to those evening conversations, some of which I did not remember fully!

Only when I moved into a "hippy" apartment in NYC did I begin to purchase wine and drink routinely, but never daily. I met my controlling husband, who drank, but not (then) alcoholically. I began to drink secretly out of a stash of wine I kept in a kitchen or bathroom cabinet. I drank very little socially, flying beneath the radar of friends and employers as a drinker. When we had wine or beer with meals, he monitored my amounts. I had a terror of driving drunk so I usually insisted on taking two cars to any social event, not drinking there, leaving early and driving home to my hidden sources to indulge! My excuse that I was an early riser was true and a good cover! Luckily, I did not suffer consequences at work or with late-night calls or other social no nos. I didn't rely on financial help or abuse friendships with dependency, as my early life had stressed that I must take care of relationships.

I first heard "my story" on a trip with a sober friend to the West Coast a year into sobriety. We stayed at a Sierra Club lodge in Nevada for a week. We hiked and went to AA meetings daily. Our leaders happened to be Buddhists!

After that, we camped along the California and Oregon coasts. A few days into our personal outing, we needed a meeting. At the desk of the youth hostel where we stayed, we found that the only meeting in the wide area started in a half-hour at a private home 25 minutes away. Zoom! Synchronicity! Hearing that someone had my exact experience was a breakthrough for me. Before this, I had felt as if I needed more ugliness and disaster to qualify as a real alcoholic!

Giving up alcohol was not a challenge for me. I did not have cravings, drunk dreams, or falters. Panic set in as I began to see my real faults hit me. My greatest needs in sobriety were to become less self-absorbed, more mature, and more fully and authentically loving. I have four awesome children and managed all the conventional mothering tasks. I was also active in my community. But, at the back of my mind, until then, there had been a focus on when I could get away with drinking one wine or beer at a meal or from my stash!

As the effects of alcohol diminished, I had more energy and attention for my children and neighborhood and was able to sponsor several women, and to feel that I could offer the wisdom of experience when I shared in meetings. For the first few years, at an assortment of conventional meetings, I did coffee and set-up service, sharing with the others who, like me, were in early sobriety. Women's meetings were important to me, as were several other meetings which went light on religious emphasis. I had two wonderful conventional sponsors, both who helped me in many ways and allowed for my non-religious life.

I look forward to the cast of characters and meaningful shared insights at my one local meeting and, occasionally, I go to several other freethinker meetings. I am committed to my Agnostic AA program.

Ed S.

I have been an atheist for 50 years and sober for 30 years. When I attended AA meetings, I initially did what everybody else did because I wanted to fit in. I said the Serenity Prayer at the beginning of meetings and the Our Father (Matthew 6: 9-15) at the end of meetings. I did most of the Steps, but could not deal with Steps Two, Three, Six and Seven. I drafted my own Steps, leaving out the God stuff. Eventually I stopped praying with the group, although I did stand in the circle, silently.

I attended a meeting in Columbus called the Meditating Peacocks. At that meeting, a woman shared how she was in AA for 10 years and struggled with the God stuff, eventually stopped going to meetings and eventually started drinking again. She explained how she lost everything, including her marriage, job and children. I thought to myself, "This should not have to happen."

After that, I looked for people at AA meetings who did not recite the Our Father after meetings, thinking they might be atheists or agnostics, also. I found two members of the Saturday Afternoon Live group. I approached them after the meeting to see if they wanted to start a non-theistic group.

We decided to meet the following week after the meeting to discuss a format for the meeting. At this time, I did not know there were other agnostic/atheist meetings in the country. There are now over 400 such meetings.

I suggested reading the Steps that I had developed years ago, but others thought that would be blasphemous, so we didn't. I am glad we decided not to use the altered steps, because I learned later that groups in Canada and Indiana were not listed in the meeting directories because they read alternate Steps. We also discussed where we would meet and agreed that it would be best if it was not in a church.

I found that Riverside Hospital had meeting rooms in their Wellness Center and they were open to us meeting there. I prepared and distributed a flyer. We held our first meeting on Jan. 4, 2011. About 20 people attended, but some of them were just curious, and some thought we were going to do a Chapter 4 of the Big Book-type meeting to persuade non-believers to come to believe.

I discovered from the Internet that there were other agnostic meetings and wrote to them asking them to send me their format. I received one from a meeting in California and we started to use that format. We met at the Wellness Center for two years until they decided to use the meeting rooms for treatment. We averaged 12-18 members.

There were several attempts to get us delisted. The first was someone who said we were affiliated with an outside group because we were listed in New York's AA Agnostic list of meetings. Next, someone said we couldn't possibly be following Tradition Two because we didn't believe in God.

We were able to deflect these and other concerns by speaking with the Advisory Board Chair of Central Ohio Group

Fellowship and our Intergroup Central Office (the body that prepares the directory of meetings). It also helped that I was on the audit committee, was also the assistant treasurer and friendly with members of the board. In addition, we have a representative from our group attend Intergroup meetings.

We moved to Dublin Hospital in 2013 and stayed there for two years, averaging 14-20 attendees. We celebrated our fourth anniversary there. Then the hospital's corporate office decided they needed the conference room for their meetings.

We now meet at St. John Lutheran Church in Dublin, Ohio. Our meeting is called Secular Sobriety.

Tomas L.

I drank my first beer when I was 16. We had a swimming pool and a sauna that we could use after PT in high school. One day, some of my classmates had brought beer. It was an amazing experience. That buzz after two or three beers was peculiar and exciting. More than that, it gave me a sense of finally finding my place in the world. I recall one of my classmates saying, "Hey Tomas, you're drunk!" It felt like the nicest compliment anyone had ever given me. I was one of the boys. I had found a place where I belonged.

When I joined AA many years later, I sometimes wondered when my addiction started. I have come to see my alcoholism as something of an addiction by proxy. It has seemed like it is not really the alcohol I want, but things like fellowship, relaxing, self confidence and relief from anxiety. It was alcohol that gave me all that, or at least an illusion of it. I had a social and emotional withdrawal that alcohol soothed. If someone would have told me there and then that I had a drinking problem, I would surely have thought them delusional. Alcohol was not the problem, it was the solution!

When I was 25 I met the woman I was to spend the next 10 years with. She was more mature and responsible than me, which meant I didn't have to bother too much about taking any responsibility. Perhaps it was mutual needs rather than love.

Drinking is what I have typically done instead of solving problems. Drinking makes problems feel less problematic, which is much easier than actually solving them. The small issues grew into big problems, which slowly but surely killed whatever love may have been between us.

When the relationship ended, I quickly went back to my bachelor style drinking. I was on a fast track bound for disaster, but was rescued by the next woman in my life after a year of bachelorhood. We fell in love and soon decided to have a baby. I had six months parental leave when my son was around one year old, and they were the most wonderful months of my life. To be with that little miracle and explore the world through his eyes was an unforgettable experience. Unfortunately, that happiness would not last. I gradually increased my drinking. As my gloom grew into a depression, I started using alcohol as self medication and ceased to even try having fun or meeting people when I drank.

In 2006 I left my job for half a year of sick leave for fatigue syndrome and depression. I went to Cognitive Behavioral Therapy and picked up my spirits enough to get back to a new job. My therapist did his best to make me realize that my drinking was a problem. I did my best at denying it.

My marriage had been going steadily downhill for years for the usual reason: drinking instead of solving problems. It took three more years before we moved apart and divorced. I resumed the pattern of drinking to numb my anxiety without any hope or intent of having fun or enjoying myself.

In August 2009 I took my first steps towards AA. I started rehab in a Minnesota Model outpatient treatment. It was there that I first said those dreaded words "I am an alcoholic." I said it mostly because the others in the group said it, but to my surprise it felt like a heavy burden was lifted off my shoulders.

That year in rehab was a very rewarding experience, but it was a strange year. The rest of my life was collapsing. The only time I felt good were those few hours in rehab once a week. My Achilles heel of sobriety has always been the feeling that my life is hopeless whatever I do. Realizing that drinking wrecks my life was easy, but believing that sobriety could give me a life worth living was far more difficult. I never really counted how many relapses I have taken, but they all started with thinking that life is a hopeless disaster either way.

I lost my job after one relapse too many in 2011. I suppose that defines me as a failure when the success rate of a treatment is calculated. I don't agree with that. I may have lost my job, but it was that year that I first admitted being an alcoholic. I found the feeling of fellowship that made me eventually stay in AA and I learned a lot about myself and alcohol. I think of it as my first important steps towards lasting sobriety. It was a very good and gentle introduction to the god bit in AA, too. As an atheist, it can be a bit of a challenge to choose my own conception of a god I don't believe in. It was fortunate that I got a non-religious introduction to AA. The leader of the meetings in rehab was very clear that there was no requirement to believe in anything but sobriety, and that God can be seen as an acronym for Fellowship Without Drugs (In Swedish: Gud = Gemenskap Utan Droger). Eventually, I found my way to a meeting. The group was very inclusive of all beliefs and lack of beliefs.

A few years of relapses alternated with a few months of sobriety. My doubts that a sober life could be a good life made my sobriety frail so it didn't take much for me to pick up that first drink. One delusion that steered me towards relapses was the idea that my alcoholism wasn't particularly progressive. I often thought of a relapse as "hitting the pause button" and taking a break from reality. My alcoholism turned out to be a standard example of the progressive type, and I discovered ways of progressiveness that I hadn't thought of. Every relapse got a bit worse than the previous. For every comeback those pink clouds of early sobriety turned more and more into something resembling the sinister darkness over Mordor.

Towards the end of 2014, I started to find new levels of darkness and despair in my depression and my drinking. My anxiety could get overwhelming in a way that I had not experienced before. There was a desperate feeling that I needed to flee in panic but didn't know where. Another sense of desperation grew from the fact that I started to lose my ability to numb my feelings with alcohol. I could dampen the desperate feeling of panic, but only to a modest level of anxiety and hopelessness. Ending my life seemed more and more like my only remaining option. To ever get a life that was even bearable seemed like a delusional dream. There were a few things that kept me from taking those thoughts to action. I did not want anyone else to suffer from my suicide, so it could not be at home. It was beyond unacceptable that my son would find my body. The thought of waking up after a failed suicide as a disabled wreck was a scary thought, so I wanted to be absolutely sure that I really died. Maybe it was some remaining survival instinct that made me complicate the plans enough to postpone them. In a way, it was one of my bad sides that helped to keep me alive: procrastination. When I had taken the edge off the worst anxiety with the first few beers, it felt less important to figure out a way to kill myself that would fit my demands, so I kept drinking and postponed it to some other day.

I gradually stopped bothering about paying any bills at all. In February 2015 I was three months behind rent and getting close to eviction. I was convinced that losing my flat would mean a one way street to a homeless life of misery that I could never return to any normal or meaningful life from. This sense that the last ship was about to sail gave me the spark for one final attempt to get sober and try to get my life back together somehow.

I had a terrible first year of sobriety. I laid the foundation for a terrible first year with all my relapses and by drinking my depression into a dark abyss.

It took about ten months until I reached a final agreement that I could keep my flat, and as I lived on social welfare I spent a lot of time collecting refund cans and bottles to fill out the gaps in my wallet and catch up with the rent. I knew I couldn't afford another relapse, so I decided to take Antabuse. It was a new level of surrender. I felt that I simply couldn't risk trusting myself and needed a crutch to stay up. I also started taking antidepressants as soon as I sobered up. To get through the worst days, I found my own dark variety of the 24 hour program: It is never too late to give up. I heard that from a comedian (Ronny Eriksson) many years ago and found a deeper, darker meaning in it. Maybe it was all hopeless and maybe all I could do was to drink myself to death, but I could at least postpone picking up the first until tomorrow. With that, the days became months.

In the spring of 2016, I sometimes felt a sense of surprised confusion. I had started my sobriety without much hope of even being alive by that spring and almost no hope of being sober that long. But there I was, alive and sober. It felt a bit like I had accidentally played some cheap trick and got away with it. My depression had gradually become less severe and I could at least have an hour or two without too much anxiety most days. I started to reflect more on how deep and horrible an abyss it was that I was climbing out of. I had learned about depression over the years. I knew that people who have had depression are prone to relapsing into depression. Looking back at the last months of drinking and first months of sobriety gave me an eerie feeling of how lost I had been and how recklessly I had stumbled along the edge of my own grave.

I started to realize that it was unlikely I would be lucky enough to survive if I were to slide back into a deeper depression. It was a scary thought that my most lethal enemy was myself. Even if I stayed sober, I knew I wasn't immune to depression. I started to feel an urge to protect me from myself, to disarm the ticking bomb that I seemed to be. It was a vague urge that I could not turn into a clear plan, but my years in and out of AA led me to the conclusion that there was at least one thing I could try. Go to meetings … lots of meetings.

My meetings had been sparse until then, maybe one meeting

a month or less. A reason for that was a sense of shame about my darkest thoughts, especially that I had thought that my own son would be better off if I was dead. I had started to realize that I was wrong about that, and felt ashamed that I could have believed something as horrible as that. The shame about that made me feel that nobody would want to have anything to do with me if they found out about my dark secret. I wasn't sure about how much I would share, but I decided that I had to at least try to go to more meetings.

It was to be the most amazing and profound experience that I have had in AA. I started to go to meetings every day, and slowly and cautiously began to come out of that closet of suicidal thoughts. At first, I would keep it brief and not get too deep or personal. I could say things like "It was hard to believe I could get a meaningful life" or "Alcohol hijacks the reward system in the brain, and that's just what it was like to me."

I didn't realize how common it really is to feel the same way I did. I believed if anyone found out about those sick, dark thoughts they would surely see me as a sick freak that they wanted nothing to do with. It was more of a feeling than anything I put words to, but I started noticing I was wrong. Nobody left the meeting when I shared or seemed to think I was weird or disgusting, so I found the courage to get more honest and explicit about my inner darkness. To my surprise and relief, what happened was the exact opposite of what I had feared. Sometimes, someone would thank me for my share after the meeting. I could often see in their eyes and hear in their voice that they had seen the same darkness as I. Others would share about similar thoughts.

I found a new level of fellowship. I wasn't nearly as different and alone as I had imagined. Gradually, I came to the insight that the dark abyss within me wasn't who I was, but something that alcohol had done to me. That insight had an amazing healing power. I'm not sure if I started something or just opened my eyes to something that was already there, but I know that spring and early summer was when I found faith. It wasn't faith in god but faith that my life could be more than just bearable. It could even be a good, meaningful and enjoyable life. After a few months, I realized that most of my days passed without any anxiety or any particularly troubling thoughts at all. My depression was gone, so by the end of the summer I stopped taking both antidepressants and Antabuse.

As I write this I am two years and nine months sober. It sometimes feels like an unbelievably long time, much longer than I thought remotely possible. That dark abyss of drinking can almost feel like a legend from long ago. And at the same time it feels like I just got started. I rarely feel any temptation to drink and often reflect on what a joy and relief it is to go through a day without having to make much of an effort to stay sober. I sometimes think of how wonderful it can be to be wrong. I thought I was a hopeless case who could not possibly stay sober more than a few months and that sobriety could not possibly be any better than just bearable. I was completely wrong about that, and I hope that I will be wrong again.

Printed in Great Britain
by Amazon